Intersectional Media

MEDIA, CULTURE, AND THE ARTS

Series Editors: Theresa Carilli and Jane Campbell,
both Purdue University Northwest

Media, Culture, and the Arts explores the ways cultural expression takes shape through the media or arts. The series initiates a dialogue about media and artistic representations and how such representations identify the status of a particular culture or community. Supporting the principles of feminism and humanitarianism, the series contributes to a dialogue about media, culture, and the arts.

Recent Titles

Intersectional Media

Representations of Marginalized Identities

Edited by
Jane Campbell
Theresa Carilli

LEXINGTON BOOKS
Lanham • Boulder • New York • London

Published by Lexington Books
An imprint of The Rowman & Littlefield Publishing Group, Inc.
4501 Forbes Boulevard, Suite 200, Lanham, Maryland 20706
www.rowman.com

6 Tinworth Street, London SE11 5AL, United Kingdom

British Library Cataloguing in Publication Information Available

Library of Congress Cataloging-in-Publication Data

Names: Campbell, Jane, 1946– editor. | Carilli, Theresa, editor.
Title: Intersectional media : representations of marginalized identities / edited by Jane
    Campbell and Theresa Carilli.
Description: Lanham : Lexington Books, [2021] | Series: Media, culture, and the arts
    | Includes bibliographical references and index. | Summary: "This book examines
    media depictions of intersecting components of marginalized identity. Through a
    study of how combined identities demonstrate a specific worldview, the contributors
    to this collection frame their understanding of media intersectionality as complex and
    multi-layered"—Provided by publisher.
Identifiers: LCCN 2021018595 (print) | LCCN 2021018596 (ebook) |
    ISBN 9781793643537 (cloth) | ISBN 9781793643520 (epub) Subjects:
LCSH: Marginality, Social. | Marginality, Social, in literature. |
    Marginality, Social, on television. | Identity (Psychology) | Intersectionality
    (Sociology)
Classification: LCC HM1136 .I67 2021 (print) | LCC HM1136 (ebook) |
    DDC 305.5/68—dc23
LC record available at https://lccn.loc.gov/2021018595
LC ebook record available at https://lccn.loc.gov/2021018596

To our parents,
Mary and Russell
and
Theresa and Umberto.

Thank you for imbuing us with a radical impulse.
And most especially to our hope that humanity will prevail and
that we will live in a world full of compassion and kindness.

J.C. and T.C.

Contents

Acknowledgments

We have spent our scholarly careers teaching and writing about the importance of understanding difference and validating the lived experiences of our students. We have met so many wonderful and brilliant individuals along the way, to whom we will always be grateful. It was a combination of luck, destiny, and a passion to heal ourselves and others. With that in mind, we would like to acknowledge our 30+ year partnership, which has resulted in scholarly collaboration.

We thank Jessica Tepper and Nicole Amstutz from Lexington Books, who have been supportive and encouraging of our vision to examine media and lived experience. Also, thanks to Mark Buckner, who has assisted us with this project.

We hope that we have contributed to creating a better world—one where the mind and the heart dictate the truth.

Introduction

Jane Campbell and Theresa Carilli

The idea of intersectionality, the lived experience of having interlocking identities, has existed for a long time. When factoring in identities involving race, gender, class, sexuality, age, religion, and ableism, intersectionality can be an extremely complex concept. When two or more identities intersect, different identities form, creating a new worldview and the potential for unique analysis. Anyone seeking to reconcile multiple identities understands the tensions that arise from this process. As early as 1903, the esteemed African American writer W.E.B. Du Bois expressed it thus: "One ever feels his twoness . . . an American, a Negro; two souls, two thoughts, two unreconciled strivings; two warring ideals in one dark body, whose strength alone keeps it from being torn asunder" (1903/2014, p. 5). In his book *The Souls of Black Folk*, Du Bois expressed his anguish about what he called this "double consciousness." Not only did he describe how these two identities affected him; he also discussed how they shaped the ways other people viewed him. For those whose lives may comprise three or even more identities, especially those that oppose the hegemonic values of society, or whose identities clash with each other, intersectionality is even more challenging.

A landmark book that announces with its very title the particular frustrations experienced by African American women is the feminist reader *All the Women Are White, All the Blacks Are Men, but Some of Us Are Brave*, edited by Akasha (Gloria T.) Hull, Patricia Bell-Scott, and Barbara Smith (1982/2015). Even today, the book remains a foundational reader for feminist studies. When it was published, its title pointed to the erasure of African American women's issues in the feminist movement, dominated by white women, in academia, in the media, in the Civil Rights movement, wherein "blacks" primarily referenced men, and in American society at large. To say that black lesbians and bisexuals were marginalized, even demonized, before

1

But Some of Us Are Brave came out is no exaggeration. This anthology changed that.

The erasure of African American women's lives persists today, despite the significant professional, academic, literary, media, and political presence of black women and the election of the first African American and South Asian American woman, Kamala Harris, to the position of vice president in 2021. As Brittney Cooper notes in her afterword to the second edition of *But Some of Us Are Brave* (2015), the wage gap between African American women and other women has widened since 1982 (p. 382). Moreover, as Cooper points out, violence against black women, both from law enforcement and against trans women, rarely receives media attention (p. 383). In 2021, issues specific to black women still deserve far more attention than they receive.

The same year Hull, Bell-Scott, and Smith's book emerged, African American poet and essayist Audre Lorde published *Zami: A New Spelling of My Name*, a memoir which she described as a biomythography (1982). In this remarkable book, part autobiography, part mythmaking, Lorde details her journey to define herself in a world confused by her multiple identities. As a lesbian, Lorde found herself accepted primarily by white lesbians for her sexuality but sometimes misunderstood or discriminated against by that community for her race. At the same time, her sexuality created tension within the black community. Adding to that, her Caribbean heritage set her apart from both communities.

The following year, renowned Marxist scholar Angela Davis published *Women, Race, and Class*, a study of the feminist movement that critiques the racial and class bias beginning during the First Wave of feminism in the United States during the nineteenth century and continuing into the Second Wave in the twentieth (1983). In 1987, Gloria Anzaldúa's *Borderlands, La Frontera: The New Mestiza* introduced some of the same concepts in her study of Mexican American women, especially queer Chicanas such as herself. Anzaldúa analyzes the feelings of Mexican Americans who live on the border between Mexico and the United States, both physically and psychologically. Many Chicano/as find themselves in a constant struggle to define themselves, given the tensions between the two countries, cultures, and languages. Each of these four books began the conversation about intersectionality, although the word did not attain currency until two years later. While intersectionality is often equated with sociological, political, and literary analysis, this book broadens the definition of intersectionality by examining identities through a media lens. By so doing, it contributes to a new understanding of the term and how it can be applied.

Most of the literature on intersectionality focuses on two issues: (1) the definition of intersectionality and (2) the methodologies and frameworks that can be used to study it. An extremely complicated and often baffling construct, intersectionality arises from feminist theory and methodology. According to Stephanie Shields (2008), intersectionality is "a central tenet of feminist thinking" (p. 301). Kimberlé Crenshaw (1989) introduced the term "intersectionality" as a way "to address legal doctrinal issues and to work both within and against the law" (Dhamoon, 2011, p. 231). Moreover, Crenshaw intended the word as a means to explore the lived experiences of black women. In her 2015 article *Intersectionality's Definitional Dilemmas*, Patricia Hill Collins (2015) expanded Crenshaw's work, arriving at the following description of intersectionality: "The term intersectionality references the critical insight that race, class, gender, ethnicity, nation, ability, and age operate not as unitary, mutually exclusive entities but as reciprocally constructing phenomena that in turn shape complex social inequalities" (p. 2).

Feminist methodologies, such as the work of Belenky and Clinchy, in *Women's Ways of Knowing* (1997), explore how lived experience foregrounds method. Women, according to this groundbreaking work, gain knowledge through experiences, and those experiences guide them in their understanding. Thus, any methodology that explores lived experience is inherently feminist. Qualitative methods, including phenomenology, are often used to study experience. Shields (2008) questions if quantitative methods work when studying intersectionality, claiming that traditional methods might simplify such a complex topic. She cites Audre Lorde's basic methodological premise, "You cannot dismantle the master's house with the master's tools" (1979). Shields notes that "the intersectional perspective is thus an invitation to move beyond one's own comfort zone" (p. 309). Other researchers have created frameworks and methods for studying intersectionality. According to Collins (2015), intersectionality could be examined as a field of study, an analytical strategy, and a form of critical praxis. Most useful to the discussion of media and intersectionality would be an analytical strategy that adopts "an intersectional way of thinking about the problem of sameness and difference and its relation to power" (Cho et al., p. 759). When talking about media representation, for example, power relations must be examined not only in terms of identity but in terms of media hegemony. Corroborating this viewpoint in their article, "Reclaiming our time: Asserting the logic of intersectionality in media studies," Joseph and Winfield write,

> Intersectionality provides a methodological tool kit that is already enriched with the subjective experiences that connect directly to the social world. That tool kit not only includes space to expand what controlling images can be but also to construct a new lens for more representative analysis. (p. 410)

While intersectionality has been referred to as "interlocking oppressions," (Collins), and "a multidimensionality of marginalized subjects' lived experiences" (Nash, p. 2), most of the literature provides frameworks to guide a study of intersectionality. Thus, intersectional analysis invites building frameworks that examine both identity and power relations. Studying intersectionality from a media perspective requires integrating the hegemony of the media with the dynamics of interlocking identities. Three key questions arise from the study of media intersectionality:

1) How can intersectionality be introduced and utilized as a framework for the study of media representations of interlocking marginalized identities?
2) Who has the authority to speak for these representations?
3) How do the power dynamics implicit in the media mitigate against the study of these marginalized representations?

As a framework for the study of media representations of interlocking marginalized identities, researchers should examine the consequences of the identities being scrutinized. How do these interlocking identities play out in the media representation? What aspects of the social worlds and the lived experiences of the individuals being represented are called into question and treated through the lens of difference? What is the language of an intersectional identity—do individuals conduct themselves in multiple realities, or through a world that contains specific cultural rules and values that demonstrate a novel and unique worldview? What information can be gleaned from the study of an intersectional representation?

As media storytellers (Hamelink, 2015), individuals who have intersectional lived experiences might be best to advocate for and explore their own oppression in media representations. As Carilli and Campbell write in their 2018 article "Gender, Ethnicity, and Religion in the Digital Age," "To adequately and sufficiently study a group of individuals who are presented in the media, individuals who have expertise and knowledge should provide a cultural context" (p. 380). In her 1976 video *Number Our Days*, ethnographer Barbara Myeroff asserted that her study of an aging Jewish community in Los Angeles was the result of her own ethnic identity. The ability to share the same worldview as those individuals she represented allowed her to give voice to this marginalized community. Myeroff was among the first ethnographers to assert that representatives from a culture are the best storytellers and analysts of that culture. While many postmodern ethnographers followed her lead (Clifford & Marcus, 1986; Marcus & Fisher, 1986), the notion that cultural members can represent themselves challenges both methodological and academic dialogue that encourages disengagement and distance from its "subjects" as a way of maintaining objectivity. Often, the best representatives of the representations are those individuals who understand a worldview and lifestyle not commonly acknowledged or represented. Individuals who study media representations can justifiably rely on these methodological arguments constructed by the postmodern ethnographers by allowing individuals with appropriate lived experience to explore interlocking identities. Methodologically, this would integrate autoethnography, the combination of autobiography and cultural experience, with media studies.

Finally, to study intersectionality and media implies having a sensitivity to the layers of the media combined with a sensitivity to the layers of multiple identities. Media hegemony, based on Gramsci's theory of ideological hegemony (Lull, p. 39), must be invoked, particularly when studying the representations and identities of marginalized/oppressed individuals. According to Boggs (1976), the mass media are tools used by the ruling elite to "perpetuate their power, wealth, and status by popularizing their own philosophy, culture, and morality" (p. 39). The media's investment in reinforcing the status quo mandates that marginalized/oppressed individuals should not have a mainstream voice in the media because that voice challenges and threatens cultural norms and values, particularly those norms and values promoting white, Anglo-Saxon values, which are the foundation of the American belief system. White male privilege, heterosexual privilege, and middle-class privilege, for example, are reified in media depictions. In the case of the January 6, 2021, insurrection on the U.S. Capitol, many journalists noted that a police presence, which was omnipresent during the 2020 #BlackLivesMatter protests, was conspicuously absent. According to CNN reporter Casey Tolan, 316 individuals protesting George Floyd's murder were arrested in Minneapolis on June 1, 2020, versus 61 individuals who were arrested on January 6, 2021, during the Capitol insurrection. Because of the composition of the mostly white male crowd during the insurrection, the media, as well as the governing institutions, did not prepare with a police or military presence. In part, this event occurred because of the belief that white men would "naturally" abide by the laws which they created. This event demonstrated a complexity never witnessed before in American history: the individuals in power whose experiences are constantly being praised for their righteousness took on a marginalized façade and created mass chaos and destruction.

At a time when the media is attempting to integrate marginalized and oppressed voices into the wider cultural dialogue, many in power are reacting with very unsettling anti-American sentiments. Studying intersectionality and media currently implies looking through the double lens of media hegemony and multilayered identity. Given this dimensional layering, we present the following articles which showcase intersectional depictions in the media.

Giovanna Del Negro's "Intersecting Dimensions of Identity in *Nonna Maria's Cantina Canadese*" explores intersections of gender, age, class, and migration status in the fictional television world of an Italian grandmother who has migrated to Canada. Nonna Maria and her millennial grandson tragi-comically explore cross-generational viewpoints that simultaneously delineate the difficulties Italian immigrants have faced in Canada and the challenges of being an aging woman in a rapidly changing world.

In "The Intersection of Race and Sexuality in Howard Cruse's *Stuck Rubber Baby*," Robert Kellerman shows that Cruse's graphic novel, set in the South during the Civil Rights Era, explores the complicated intersections African American and white queer characters face. Kellerman's analysis reveals surprising twists in the novel that belie expectations about sexuality and race.

Katrina Webber and Layla Cameron's "A Work in Progress: Advancing Intersectionality In and Through Queer Television" compares the series *The L Word* (2004-2009) and its 2019 reboot *Generation Q* with *Work in Progress*, another series premiering in 2019. Webber and Cameron argue that while *Generation Q* demonstrates more inclusivity and currency in its depictions of the LGBTQ+ community than *The L Word*, *Work in Progress* offers far more awareness of intersectional, dimensional characters and viewpoints, showing greater sensitivity to class, race, sexuality, gender, mental health, and disability.

In "Race, Poverty, and Narco-capitalism on *The Wire*: A Political Economic Analysis," Michael Johnson explores intersectionality in the acclaimed HBO drama. Johnson examines the hierarchy that exists in all aspects of the narcotics industry, demonstrating the complex ways *The Wire* represents race, poverty, and class through its characters and plots.

In "The Transgender Super Nanny, *Babysitter Gin*: A Postcolonial Analysis," Kimiko Akita explores the intersectional identities of a Japanese "super nanny" dressed like Mary Poppins, who is named "Gin." Gin first emerged as a *manga* (comic book) character and was rebooted as a live actor in a TV series based on the original storylines. Akito asserts that both versions of Gin appeal to a female audience partly because they embody the intersections of femininity and masculinity.

Theresa Carilli's chapter "The Intersection Between Ethnicity, Gender, and Class in the HBO series, *My Brilliant Friend*: The Cost of Defiance and Resistance" focuses on how the two central characters, Elena and Lila, forge identities in a world that strives to crush their spirits as they move from childhood to adulthood in 1950s Naples. Carilli explores the ways *My Brilliant Friend* taps into her ancestral memory, furthering her understanding of her intersectional culture and her own struggles to accept and transcend it.

Sara Raffel and Amanda Hill's chapter "UpWord Mobility: The Intersection of Rhetorics, Hip Hop, and History in *Hamilton: An American Musical*" examines creator Lin-Manuel Miranda's work as a revisioning of U.S. history. Through celebrating racially diverse cultures, working-class characters, "street" vernacular, and hip-hop to tell Hamilton's story, Miranda reframes political resistance to reach a wide audience.

In "Kim Chi at RuPaul's Drag Race: Rearticulating Fatphobia, Sissyphobia, and Asianphobia in the Gay Male Community in American Context," Quang Ngo demonstrates how drag queen Kim Chi embraces her uniqueness. Ngo argues that even in an arena that privileges white, ultramasculine, thin drag performers, Kim Chi embraces her own full-figured, feminine Korean self, refusing to allow herself to be marginalized.

Maha Bashri examines media intersectionality through a political lens. In "Framing the Democratic Socialists of America? National and Local Information Flows in Media Coverage of Alexandria Ocasio-Cortez," Bashri notes that media coverage of female political figures, specifically Ocasio-Cortez, most often focuses on personal rather than policy issues. By using media framing as a research tool to study intersectionality with respect to gender, race, and class, Bashri concludes that media primarily focused on her class background.

We offer this collection as a foray into media depictions of intersectionality. With this book, we hope to foster a multilayered dialogue about identity. By so doing, we seek to provoke further exploration.

REFERENCES

Anzaldúa, G. (1987). *Borderlands: The new Mestiza: La frontera.* Aunt Lute Books.

Belenky, M., & Clinchy, B. M. (1997). *Women's ways of knowing: The development of self, voice, and mind* (Tenth Anniversary Edition). Basic Books.

Boggs, C. (1976). *Gramsci's Marxism.* Plato Press.

Carilli, T., & Campbell, J. (2020). Gender, ethnicity, and religion in the digital age. In Y. Kamalipour (Ed.), *Global communication: A multicultural perspective* (Third Edition). Rowman & Littlefield.

Cho, S., Crenshaw, K. W., & McCall, L. Toward a field of intersectionality studies: Theory, applications, and praxis. *Signs, 38*(4), 785–810.

Clifford, J., & Marcus, G. (1986). *Writing culture: The poetics and politics of ethnography.* University of California Press.

Collins, P. H. (2015). Intersectionality's definitional dilemmas. *The Annual Review of Sociology, 41*(1), 1–20.

Collins, P. H., & Blige, S. (2016). *Intersectionality.* Polity.

Crenshaw, K. (1989). Demarginalizing the intersection of race and sex: A black feminist critique of antidiscrimination doctrine, feminist theory, and antiracist politics. *University of Chicago Legal Forum, 1*, 139–167.

Davis, A. (1983). *Women, race, and class.* Penguin.

Dhamoon, R. K. (2011). Considerations on mainstreaming intersectionality. *Political Research Quarterly, 64*(1), 230–243.

Du Bois, W. E. B. (2014). *The souls of black folk*. Create Space Independent Publishing Platform. (Original work published 1903).

Gramsci, A. (1978). *Selections from cultural writings*. Harvard University Press.

Hamelink, C.J. (2015). *Global communication.* Sage.

Hull, A, (G. T.), Bell-Scott, P., & Smith, B. (*2015*). *All the women are white, all the blacks are men, but some of us are brave* (Second Edition). Feminist Press. (Original work published 1982).

Joseph, J. L., & Winfield, A.S. (2019). Reclaiming our time: Asserting the logic of Intersectionality in media studies. *Women's Studies in Communication, 42*(4), 408–411.

Lorde, A. (1979, September 29). *The master's tools will never dismantle the master's house*. [Comments at the 'Personal and Political Panel']. The Second Sex—Thirty Years Later. New York University.

Lorde, A. (1982). *Zami: A new spelling of my name: A biomythography*. Crossing Press.

Lull, J. (1995). *Media, communications, and culture: A global approach*. Columbia University Press.

Marcus, G., & Fischer, M. (1986). *Anthropology as cultural critique: An experimental moment in the human sciences*. University of Chicago Press.

Myeroff, B., & Kaminsky, M. (2007). *Stories as equipment for living: Last talks and tales of Barbara Myeroff*. University of Michigan Press.

Nash, J.C. (2008). "Re-thinking intersectionality." *Feminist Review, 89*(1), 1–15.

Shields, S.A. (2008). "Gender: An intersectional perspective." *Sex Roles, 59*(1): 301–311.

Tolan, C. (2021, January 9). *D.C. police made far more arrests at the height of the Black Lives Matter protests than during the capitol clash*. CNN. Retrieved January 11, 2021, From https://www.cnn.com/2021/01/08/us/dc-police-arrests-blm-capitol-insurrection-invs/index.html

Chapter 1

Intersecting Dimensions of Identity in *Nonna Maria's Cantina Canadese*

Giovanna P. Del Negro

With over 600,000 views, the YouTube video *Nonna Maria's Cantina Canadese* (2009c) is tremendously popular among young Italian ethnics in Montreal today. Posted on the YouTube channel *Nonna Maria's TV*, the video is set in the iconic Italian immigrant *cantina* (food cellar), with its bottled tomato puree, pickled vegetables, and aging *prosciutto*. Videos on the channel feature the irrepressible titular character, a cloth puppet who comes to life through the puppeteer's unique use of vernacular and malapropisms. Here, creator Anthony Imperioli comically captures an indelibly Italian-Canadian form of speech, which borrows heavily from rich southern Italian dialects, French Québécois, and English. In so doing, he renders for his audience the complex feelings elderly Italian immigrants have toward their homeland and the new generation.

This chapter explores the ways in which gender, age, class, and migration status intersect, combine, overlap, and conflict in the fictional world of this linguistically challenged *nonna* (grandmother) and her millennial grandson. Ultimately, I seek to understand how Nonna performs the deeply interconnected aspects of her identity and what these subject positions tell us about power relations, marginalization, and social exclusion in the wider context of the post-WWII mass migration of Italians to Canada and the struggle for French language rights in Quebec. As I will show, gender expectations in Italian immigrant culture change across the person's lifecycle, and the role of the *nonna* is a complex one, with cross-cutting privileges and disadvantages. Indeed, the immigrant *nonna* is not only valued for her knowledge and wisdom, but for her courage to leave her home behind in search of better prospects. With age, the working-class *nonna*, with her southern dialect and irreverent style of interaction, is blissfully free from the pressures to attract a husband, raise children, and conform to traditional images of feminine desirability. As a result, she enjoys greater freedom of expression, even as she experiences a decline in physical and mental abilities. The first part of this chapter provides a detailed description of the *Nonna Maria Cantina Canadese* video, as well as background information on the creator and the Italian community in Montreal, while the second part will analyze the representation of the elderly *nonna* from an intersectional perspective. Nonna Maria's character can only be understood in the context of Italian immigrant women's lives, and throughout the chapter, I will tack back and forth between the video text I analyze and the social historical climate in which that text is made meaningful.

Systems of inequality and oppression rooted in ethnic discrimination, chronic otherness, male hegemony, linguistic conflict, and the hidden injuries of class have profoundly marked the experiences of Italian immigrant women of the post-war generation. But like the Italian working-class immigrant women she represents, Nonna Maria is more than the sum total of the subordination and exploitation she has endured. Quite the contrary, she is an indomitable force of nature. An instigator of fun and levity, she defiantly rejects the veneration of Italian culture that so often comes at the expense of Italian immigrants, who are often judged by those from the home country as having lost their culture, accusing them of being inauthentically Italian. It is a cruel irony of diaspora that Italy's post-war reconstruction depended on the money that those disparaged immigrants sent home to their more "authentic" cousins. For many second- and third-generation Italians in Montreal and other places in the diaspora, the Nonna Maria's videos are an invitation to let our guard down, to name and own our experiences as we laugh, and to enjoy the difference that has helped make us who we are.

Set against a backdrop of homemade wine, bottles of tomato preserve, *giardiniera* (pickled vegetables), aging cheese and *prosciutto*, and store-bought items, we see Nonna Maria's straining to hold a fixed pose, only to keel over with exhaustion while she nudges her grandson to take the photograph. Nonna, who is mildly irritated, tells him, "*David, David, prend, prend a foto, stai a prende a photo?*" (David, David, take the photo, take the photo, are you taking the photo?), but she soon realizes that he is shooting video instead of taking still pictures. Fast on the uptake, Nonna responds with a good-natured quip, "*Ah, hai visto, che bella technologia.*" (Ah, you see, what wonderful technology.) She then proceeds to give everyone in "Italia" a warm hello, with special greetings for Assunta and Teresa and "*tutti quando*" (everyone) while she bobs her head from side to side, blowing kisses saying "I love you, I love you, I love you." Rushed along by her impatient grandson, she proudly begins her tour of la cantina Canadese by first pointing to the homemade *caccio cavallo* (aged cheese). Turning her attention to the tomato preserves, Nonna says, "*Quest e lu sugo, tomoto, che siammo fatto noi, semme fatto solo*

uno peche tutto l'altre seme fata scape endere tutto, David a scapete sotto."
(This is for sauce, tomato sauce, which we made; we only have one because
all the rest David dropped on the floor.) Nonna, who is still upset with David,
blurts out, "*Va fa cullo*" (Go f—yourself). David, who tries to shrug off any
responsibility, says, "*Non e colpa mia*" (It isn't my fault), but Nonna, who has
the upper hand with the revelation of her grandson's ineptitude, warns him
to be quiet. She says, "*Oke sta zito David, stonga a parla.*" (Okay, David, be
quiet, I am speaking.) A chastised David mutters an apology, but Nonna has
already moved onto the vacuum-packed sausages which she is gently stroking. Speaking in a soft, hushed tone Nonna says, "*Sai queste, le salsice qua,
bella salcie Canadese, hai visto, hai vista, come bella, queste sai*" (You know
these sausages, nice Canadian sausages, can you see, can you see how beautiful they are, well these sausages you know), when David suddenly loses
control of the camera. Unphased, Nonna resumes her story about her husband Luigi's unwholesome attraction to sausages. In a surprising act of self-
restraint, Nonna places her hands over her mouth to censure herself, "*Oke,
Oke, state ziti, Maria.*" (Okay, okay, don't speak, Maria.) Eager to change the
subject, Nonna gestures toward the bag of Tostitos in the pantry which she
claims are homemade, in her words, "*qualche cose che seme fatta noi, fate di
casa.*" (something that we made, homemade.) Her grandson David, knowing
full well that Nonna is being insincere, says, "Come on Nonna, don't lie, you
didn't make the Tostitos, *yam*" (dialect for "come on"). Feigning outrage at
her grandson's insolence and trying to deflect attention away from her white
lie, Nonna accuses him of being a know-it-all, a young whippersnapper who
thinks he knows better than his elders. Raising her voice and waving her arms
back and forth to register her displeasure, Nonna admonishes David: "*Eye
oke, oke, David tu sai tutto, David, tu sai tutto.*" (Ay, okay, okay David. You
know everything, David, you know everything.)

By the time Nonna nears the end of her tour she is ever pluckier and mis-
chievous. Pointing to her husband's wine she says, "*Queste e o vino, e o vino,
ma fatto Luigi, pero sa d'acetto*" (This wine was made by Luigi, but it tastes
of vinegar) and lets out a raucous laugh. Nonna attempts to reign in her harsh
comments; she hems and haws about the merits of Luigi's wine, "*Sai pech u
vino e nu poco, oke va fan culo, va*" (You know the wine is a little—okay, f—
it) but eventually gives in to brutal honesty and curses at her inability to spare
her husband's feelings. After a momentary loss of composure, Nonna turns
to the store-bought supply of tomato paste in her cantina and tells her public
back home, "*Quest la comprama, e u 'Pastena' tomato juice.*" (This we buy.
It is Pastena tomato juice.) David corrects his grandmother and tells her, "No,
it's just paste, tomato paste, Nonna," but Nonna, who misunderstands he is
making fun of the whole situation, says, "Toothpaste, toothpaste?" David,
who is exasperated by this point says, "*No, no, toothpaste, per lava i denti*

. . . *tomato paste per il sugo.*" (No, no, toothpaste is to brush your teeth! Tomato paste is for sauce.) Waving her hand back and forth over her mouth in a brushing motion and comically contemplating the absurdity of cleaning one's teeth with tomato juice, Nonna says, "Mmh, mmh, tomato, mmh, mmh tomato."

The Nonna Maria character originated with prank phone calls that Imperioli as a teenager made to the Leonardo Da Vinci Italian Cultural Community Center in Montreal which is frequented by Italian senior citizens and evolved into a series of videos that have become enormously popular in Canada, with the most-watched segments reaching over 600,000 hits. Imperioli serves as the puppeteer in these videos, which are either improvised or lightly scripted. His longtime childhood friend David Iarusso plays the part of David, and Ermine Crapanzano plays Nonna Maria's husband Chef Luigi, while Imperioli's girlfriend Melissa Salveggio occasionally pitches in to help with production and filming. The sketches have clearly struck a chord with Montreal's Italian ethnic community, and Nonna Maria's success depends on Imperioli's ability to skillfully capture and exaggerate the kinesics and behavior that we might associate with an aging "cute" Italian immigrant woman of her generation. Across his many videos, Imperioli plays for laughs the squinting, coughing, aphasic pauses, and mispronunciations (e.g., "penis" instead of "pennies," "Hallowinga" to refer to Halloween) of an Italian grandmother without filters. The limitations of puppet Nonna, who is devoid of fingers and human hair, are also fodder for comedy. At her neighborhood ethnic salon, Nonna's hairstylist, who code-switches between Italian, French, and English without batting an eye, tells her that she could benefit from un *rivitalisant* (conditioner) to "*amorbidire*" (softener) for her desiccated, unruly mop of hair. Here, the unruly mop of hair is literally a small-scale, puppet-size mop with straggly twisted ends and a knot on top, which she has neatly tucked into a bun (Nonna Maria's TV, 2010).

In *Nonna Maria's Cantina Canadese*, what starts off as a loving video postcard to family and friends paradoxically degenerates into a litany of complaints and repressed grievances. Immigrant feelings of inferiority, longing for home, and a sense that their sacrifices and achievements haven't been properly recognized are covered by bold assertions of the immigrants' superiority, and the choice to leave one's place of birth is justified by the lavish display of the cantina, which holds prized food and delicacies. Among the second wave of Italian immigrants who settled in Montreal in the post-WWII era, the cantina is understood as a mythic land of plenty, overflowing with the wine, cheese, and bounty of the earth (Del Giudice, 2001). In this gastronomical utopia, hunger is banished, and the *miseria* (hunger) that prompted so many Italians to leave home is assuaged by a well-stocked pantry that can fend off the food insecurity brought on by war or natural disaster. It is no accident that Nonna's grandson is charged with documenting this part of the Italian home, given its significance in Italian immigrant culture. The straight man to Nonna's antics, David is often made to look the fool for his stupidity and lack of judgment, whether it involves his habit of sleeping late or his enjoyment of French-Canadian fast food such as *poutine*—a common Québécois dish (originating from the Canadian province of Quebec) made with French fries, gravy, and cheese curds (Nonna Maria's TV, 2009a). The litany of demands, sarcastic remarks, and complaints directed at David, however, are rooted in love and affection. Despite the generational chasm, David and Nonna Maria enjoy spending time together, and the bond between the two becomes readily apparent in the episode in which David has a nightmare about the disappearance of his grandmother, an episode that I will discuss later.

In many ways, *Nonna Maria's Cantina Canadese* is a loving parody of a style of interaction that grows out of a sense of immigrant uncertainty and ambivalence toward both the later generational ethnics in Montreal and to those Italians who never left their homeland—those whose economic progress was significantly fueled by the loyalty and monetary support of millions of displaced diaspora Italians like Nonna Maria. Indeed, that economic progress is so great today that it has attracted a steady stream of migrants from Morocco, the Philippines, Tunisia, Albania, Nigeria, Senegal, Ghana, and Somalia who have come to Italy to work and in turn send remittances back to *their* families. Italians who live in Italy today can claim the authenticity of the home country that Italian immigrants often feel they are excluded from asserting. Nonna refuses to participate in the veneration of Italian culture that comes at the expense of Italian immigrants, Italian immigrants who sent money back home to help rebuild the home country's economy that those who didn't leave so proudly celebrate. While Quebec society can't boast the 2,000 years of culture and history the Italians enjoy nor compete with France in terms of status and visibility—indeed Quebec is often referred to as *les petit cousins de l'Amérique* relative to France—the Italian ethnic identity parodied in Imperioli's YouTube episode valorizes and pays homage to immigrant creativity, resourcefulness, tenacity, and poetry, which is evoked in the speech, gestures, and arts of *argangarsi* (making do) that Nonna Maria has come to represent.

In the midst of a patriarchal Italian culture that often relegates women to the margins of society, Anthony Imperioli, a third-generation Italian ethnic male, has created an older female character who not only occupies center stage but makes men the butt of her jokes. By inverting traditional gender relations and refusing to be quiet or obedient, Imperioli has found in Nonna Maria's unique vernacular a transgressive expression of feminist humor and female *jouissance* (joy, enjoyment) Italian style. As a second-generation Italian from Montreal, Nonna Maria epitomizes the cultural practices and expressive styles—linguistic, gestural, and interactional—that have helped define the identity and flavor of today's Italian community in Montreal. With the ever-greater assimilation and acceptance of Italians in Quebec society, the markers of difference—food, language, balconies turned into vegetable gardens, wine making, cantinas, *bocce* playing, and even Italian-Canadian speech patterns that borrow heavily from rich Central and southern dialects, Québécois, and English—today are sources of pride, rather than shame. The immigrant culture of our *nonna*, once enjoyed in private at a safe distance from the judgmental gaze of others, can now be relished on the widely public platform of YouTube. This historically de-valorized culture of post-WWII Italian immigrants from Montreal who have been made to feel inferior, backward, and uncivilized can now be parodied with love and affection, and wistfully evoke a nostalgia of an era that is about to pass but is still audible.

What can we learn by exploring the ways in which gender, ethnicity, class, and age interact and shape the representations of the Nonna character from Imperioli's YouTube creation? Do the predicaments in which Nonna finds herself have any connection to the situations which an older Italian woman might encounter in her everyday life? By analyzing the relationship between a linguistically challenged Italian immigrant grandmother and her third-generation Italian millennial grandson, we ultimately discover that gender expectations and perceptions of Italian women change as they move from one stage of life to another. The real-life, younger, working-class Maria from Imperioli's symbolic universe, based on the historical record of Italian immigrant women of this period, could have spent the better part of her existence working in a garment factory, struggling to meet daily quotas, and tending to husband, children, and domestic chores. If the fictional Maria were not earning wages in the formal economy, she might find herself supplementing her husband's income by starting a home business as a seamstress, minding other people's children, and engaging in various forms of women's labor in the home, which benefited the family financially and emotionally—sewing outfits for children, doing embroidery, making tomato puree, pickling vegetables, and maintaining social ties with kinfolk. The older Nonna, however, has copious amounts of leisure time to devote to her hair-brained schemes and is more interested in causing mayhem than she is in catering to her husband. Most of all, however, the *nonna*, by virtue of her age, is blissfully unburdened by the pressures of heteronormativity. Because she has passed her sexual prime, is no longer capable of bearing children, and out of the marriage market because she has a spouse, she is under no obligation to find a mate or make herself desirable to members of the opposite sex. What Maria loses in status and power for her inability to procreate she makes up for with her role as the immigrant *nonna*.

The immigrant *nonna* not only commands respect and admiration, as she enters her twilight years, she also enjoys greater freedom of expression and is less bound by narrow visions of Italian femininity. The *nonna* in Italian culture is widely revered for her longevity, cultural knowledge, and the perceived wisdom that comes with age. In the context of the ethnic environment in Montreal, what is deserving of highest praise is Nonna's immigrant sacrifice—learning a new language, navigating an urban environment that has historically been hostile to Italians, and feeling homesick for the food, language, and warm embrace of the people that she left behind. The immigrant Nonna has not only survived the devastation of WWII Italy but the challenges of starting a new life in a place that is as far geographically, climatically, and culturally as anything that she has ever known. With age, however, Nonna Maria is entitled to speak more freely and in ways that would be considered inappropriate for a young unmarried Italian adolescent girl of her generation. Hence, the older *Nonna* enjoys privileges that a younger Maria does not; she can speak her mind unrestrained by the values of middle-class decorum, whether it means chiding her grandson for his lack of culinary taste or expressing resentment toward family back home who find her hybrid Italian immigrant culture at best amusing, and at worst, warped and inauthentic. However, the greater cultural tolerance for the outspoken, defiant, and even transgressive behavior of the geriatric *nonna* by comparison to her younger counterpart doesn't mean that Italian women who have yet to be grandmothers are by definition quiet, docile, or powerless.

The often culturally restrictive climate in which Italian immigrant women were raised no doubt shaped the way they conceived of their obligations to their family and the wider community, but the lived experience of these women is more complicated than we might think. "While the husband is considered the 'pater familias,' exercising his authority over his wife and children, both legally and by accepted custom" studies show that the women controlled the purse strings of the family and made important decisions about children's education and career choices (Bonar, 1996, p. 68). Indeed, Bonar reveals that the older Italian immigrant women in her study did not see themselves as passive housewives who simply deferred to the men in their lives. In fact, large numbers of Italian immigrants of the period because of economic necessity found themselves joining the labor force for the first time, and with their wage-earning capacity came a greater sense of independence and a "perception of the relationship between husband and wife as one of equal partnership" (Bonar, 1996, p. 68). The migration experience, with all its hardship, served an emancipatory role for some by loosening the grip of patriarchy, which sought to confine women to the private sphere. The newly acquired wage-earning ability of Italian immigrant women, however, came with greater demands on their time: a double workday, one at the factory and another at home. The Canadian economy benefited greatly from the cheap labor of the mass influx of Italian immigrants who arrived in Montreal after WWII. The unskilled, low-paying jobs for which Italian immigrant women were hired during the economic boom of 1960s Montreal helped provide stable and reliable employment.

The Italian grandmother of the Nonna Maria universe is filled with youthful exuberance as she bobs around the screen with excitement, yet the declining mental faculties and physical limitations that are tied to her advanced age, and the fact that Nonna is a puppet, sometimes clouds her judgment and her ability to navigate the universe in ways that humans can. In the aforementioned scene in which David corrects his grandmother for referring to a can of "Pastena" brand tomato paste as tomato juice, Nonna, a nonnative-English speaker, cannot fully grasp the difference between the two. Lunacy ensues as she humorously contemplates the ideas of tomato-flavored toothpaste by motioning across her mouth, as if brushing her teeth, and making noises of satisfaction, which betray her true meaning, as she says, "Mmh, mmh, toothpaste, mmh, mmh, toothpaste." While one can easily chalk up this incident to linguistic misunderstanding, it is clear from David's interactions with his Nonna that she has difficulty listening and following his rather simple line of reasoning—that on the one hand there is *sugo* (sauce), which is made from tomato puree, and that on the other hand, there is tomato paste, a thickening agent used in sauce, which is different from toothpaste, even though they both sound the same. One could argue that Nonna is too impatient to think through the tomato paste/tomato juice dilemma; however, there are moments in the series in which Nonna is clearly struggling with cognitive-related issues and appears stuck in a quasi-aphasic trance with her mouth open as if she is to speak, but no words come out. At one visit to the hair salon, Nonna sits down to leaf through a magazine but is incapable of doing so because the Nonna puppet lacks proper fingers. While this scene is played for laughs, it touches on the decreased manual dexterity that people experience as they get older. Moreover, the problems that Nonna the puppet encounters as she seeks to perform human-like behavior in a world that fails to respond accordingly is not unlike the problems older people experience with bodies that no longer work in the ways that they are meant to work. How much of Nonna's hazy thinking and distractibility are rooted in declining health related to age, or a disinterest in mastering a language that she will never have to use, or her zealous desire to take in as much of the world as possible with the limited time she has left, we will never fully know, but watching a puppet attempt to express the gestural repertoire of an Italian *nonna* is indeed fodder for comedy.

But there is more going on here than silly slapstick. As the producer and show runner for the videos, Imperioli creatively exploits the limits of puppetry to produce a complex portrayal of age embodiment. Here, the flesh-and-blood grandson displays forms of physical agility that the cloth-and-foam Maria does not possess, and the contrast between the two dramatizes the effects of aging on the human body. Though puppetry is understood as a form of high culture in some cultures, in North America and Europe it is usually understood as a comic form, one appropriate only for children (or at least light-hearted topics), not serious cultural reflection. This framing allows Imperioli to explore the life-and-death issues of aging in a nonthreatening manner, and David, who serves as caretaker and comedic sidekick, is all too aware of his *nonna*'s increasing mental and physical fragility, as well as her imminent demise. The age of Nonna is never revealed, but if I could hazard a guess, she is probably in her 70s or early 80s. Further, puppets have a more limited expressive range than flesh-and-blood humans, and the Nonna Maria videos take advantage of this to produce a complex effect. An actor on the stage can present the audience with hundreds of subtly distinct facial expressions, and with close-up shots, the actor in a movie or video can portray countless complex emotions with the subtlest facial gestures. In contrast, the puppeteer may only move the puppet's mouth, body, and arms, but this very limitation offers a unique set of interpretive possibilities. As Emmanuel Levinas (1961/1969) has observed, in embodied encounters, we directly *see* in the face of the other an infinite possibility for interaction and response. When we suspend disbelief in a theatrical or filmic performance, we perceive the body of the actor as a character that has just exactly that kind of depth: that is, we see the actor's face as a site of the character's deep well of interiority and vast potential for new reactions. But when we see a puppet, we must suspend two layers of disbelief—that the puppet is a subject (not an object made of cloth and foam) and that that subject isn't the product of the performer's artifice but a person with an interiority and agency. Putting a puppet at the center stage, the Nonna Maria videos give us a unique perspective on the nature of expressivity and aging. Looking at Nonna Maria, we are reminded how age dampens our facial expressivity, but also the ways in which a depth of experience may lurk beneath the relatively less mobile face of the aging other

The growing dependence of aging populations on family and the support systems for their well-being are well established, but what is interesting about the Nonna Maria videos is that the young millennial grandson watches over his grandmother, helping her navigate the modern world and playing "second banana" to an aging Italian immigrant woman who is anything but invisible, isolated, or quiet. David's concern for his *Nonna*'s safety is palpable in one episode in which he has a dreadful nightmare that Nonna has gone missing (Nonna Maria's TV, 2011b). David is so distraught that he can be seen posting pictures of his grandmother around town with the hope of learning about her whereabouts. In the horror-inspired scene, David is inconsolable; he mopes around the house aimlessly, unable to make himself a proper plate of pasta, when suddenly the nightmare comes to an end, and he awakens with Nonna by his side gently stroking his face and reassuring him that all is well. The idea that David's pasta-making skills or appetite for pasta disappears at the same time that his grandmother does is both poignant and funny. Without Nonna by his side, providing guidance and support, David cannot bring himself to eat the Italian dish. For David, Nonna is not only the cultural bearer of Italian knowledge that keeps him connected to his ethnic identity but a source of comfort on which he has come to depend, despite her intrusions and grumbling. The humor of this scene, however, lies in the fact that the loss of the *nonna* is so great that it can displace a culinary tradition that has become synonymous with Italian culture, thereby making pasta and human life of commensurate importance. Here, the potential loss of Nonna implies a threat to the very foodways which keep Italian identity alive. However, at the same time David bemoans the disappearance of his grandmother, he also bemoans her technological ineptitude and lack of interest in mainstream popular culture. The tutorials he gives his *nonna* on how to operate the DVD player (Nonna Maria's TV, 2011a) are as unsuccessful as his attempts to teach her about the wonders of the Super Mario Brothers (Nonna Maria's TV, 2009b).

A millennial in his late twenties, David lives with his nonna in what looks like a basement apartment. While many Italian immigrant women supported homeownership as a means of financial independence and class mobility, they were by no means middle-class in their educational attainment or lifestyle. Most of the Italian women who immigrated to Montreal in the post-World War II era came from impoverished small towns in southern Italy and lacked formal education. They were largely of the peasantclass who stopped going to school at a young age and spent time helping with domestic chores that included daily long walks to the well and communal fountains to retrieve drinking water and launder clothes, seeding, picking, and selling crops from small estates, or learning to apprentice as seamstresses (Ramirez, 1989; Iacovetta, 1993). The homes that Italian immigrant families often preferred were buildings that could offset the cost of the mortgage—tri-plexes or five-plexes with three or five rental units which could generate income and accommodate multiple generations under one roof. For the Italian immigrant family, homeownership meant financial security, a buffer against difficult economic times, a modicum of wealth they could pass onto their children, and a nest egg for their retirement years. But the dream of owning a small "Casetta in Canada" ["House in Canada"] (Pizzi, 1957), a popular Italian song about the immigrant hope of owning a small home with a backyard, could only be achieved after a lifetime of sacrifice and a modest lifestyle, which generally didn't include regular vacations, except for the occasional trips to Italy and forms of amusement that focused largely on socializing with relatives and *paesani*, kinfolk from the same village. Therefore, it is no accident that most of the action from Nonna Maria's videos occurs in private, intimate spaces of working-class immigrant sociability where Nonna feels at ease—kitchens, living rooms, ethnic grocery stores, and hair salons, where employees are adept at speaking to Nonna in her own mélange of Italian and French.

The working-class status of Nonna, however, is epitomized by her southern dialect and her lack of middle-class visions of female decorum. If Nonna had received a more formal education, she probably would be speaking in standard Italian, the language of elite, privileged Italians who benefited from attending institutions of advanced learning in faraway urban centers. Moreover, Nonna does not possess any middle-class reserve; she is assertive, loud, and unconcerned with the rules of turn-taking or polite conversation. Indeed, she can usually be seen gesticulating wildly, speaking over David, and defiantly rejecting the superiority he or others wield over her because she is perceived as old-fashioned or lacking in sophistication and Italian authenticity. In *Nonna Maria's Cantina Canadese*, Nonna refers to her *"Quebekquick prosciutto"* (*prosciutto* made in Quebec) as the best in the world. David, who scoffs at his grandmother, tells her that Italian-made *prosciutto* is far better than immigrant-made prosciutto. Nonna, tired of the veneration of Italy's savoir faire that comes at the expense of Italian immigrants, digs in her heels, and says in the tone of a toddler who is about to throw a tantrum, "No, ours [*prosciutto*] is better than theirs [in Italy]." David, who unsuccessfully tries to disabuse his grandmother of the ludicrousness of this idea, is chastised by Nonna, who tells her know-it-all grandson, while waving her arms back and forth for dramatic effect, "You know everything, you know everything." David, who refuses to yield, in turn accuses Nonna of being a showoff, and Nonna, who is visibly upset, raising her voice, says, "I'm not a 'show wop!' They are, those stupid people who never want to send us money, here." David tries to correct his grandmother's mispronunciation of "show off," but ultimately Nonna gets the last word. In this heated exchange with all of Nonna's signature malapropisms, Nonna feels disrespected by her entitled grandson, who snobbishly touts the superiority of Italian culture over that of Italian immigrant culture without fully appreciating the contributions of Italian immigrants to Canadian society or the frugal lifestyle of early Italian immigrants which made it possible to send money back home to help to rebuild their economically ravaged villages. In this situation, Nonna is being yet again marginalized. However, it is not from the industrialized Northern part of Italy which has historically blamed the South—people from her own region—for its poverty and social ills, the xenophobes who told her to go home when she first arrived, but from her very own grandson, who privileges the culinary contributions of Italy to the world over that of the more pedestrian foodways and culture of Italian immigrants like Nonna.

Nonna's working-class identity, however, also is expressed through her playfully irreverent style of interaction, which many women of her generation often enjoyed during moments of female sociability. For many working-class Italian immigrant women, the transgressive joke-telling, irreverent verbal banter, and mock swearing often occurred on the factory floor to help with the tedium of work and foster a sense of female solidarity (Del Negro, 2004). The expressive repertoire of Nonna is not only deeply rooted in her immigrant experience, but it is also deeply gendered, classed, and developed in the female-dominated context of working-class spaces. While such behavior flouts middle-class visions of female propriety, Nonna's shouting, cursing, argumentativeness, and passive aggressive statements, which are meant in jest, could be seen as a desire to be heard by those who are not listening or paying older people any attention. To the Italian notables of her community at home and abroad, she is a quaint old Italian immigrant woman who clings to antiquated notions of Italian culture and lives on the borders of Italian and Canadian society. Nonna Maria is not *not* Italian; she was born in Italy and now claims Montreal as her home, but she is also not fully Canadian or a dyed-in-the-wool Québécoise, despite her naturalization. She is betwixt and between, a cartoonish, liminal figure who shouts and curses at her grandson's refusal to wear a jacket, for example. David doesn't pay heed to his grandmother's warning to bundle up against hostile elements, which if seen through a historical lens could be metaphorically understood as a warning against ethnic hostilities that have shaped Italian Quebec relations from the 1950s and the early 2000s. Likewise, the tomato puree debacle, which still angers Nonna to this day, could be read as a commentary on the cavalier attitude that young Italian ethnics like David display toward the older immigrant culture of people like his *nonna*. In the first scenario, the *nonna* is an overprotective maternal figure, while the second scenario symbolically highlights the grandson's lack of awareness that bottles of tomato puree made by Nonna are fragile, as fragile as his ethnic identity, which hangs by a tenuous thread.

The perception of Italians as inferior, and the interethnic conflicts which existed between the Italians and the Québécois, are well documented. Italians were considered nonpreferred immigrants: a swarthy, dirty lot, unassimilable foreign others accused of stealing Canadian jobs (Mastracci, 2018). The women and children joining their husbands who had arrived first in Montreal were only allowed to enter as dependents who were deemed the responsibility of husbands, and their status as dependents made them ineligible for assistance or training programs (Iacovetta, 1993). The early Italian immigrant women of the period experienced discrimination, as did their children. Not only do they remember being called *maudis Italien*, *voleurs de job* (damned Italians, job stealers), and *wops*, but their children were refused entry into the French schools, which sought to maintain French cultural homogeneity. The tensions between Italian immigrants and the Québécois came to a boil in the late 1960s when residents of the largely Italian community of St. Leonard rioted against plans to turn the English school that their children attended into a unilingual French school in order to curb the low birthrate among French-Canadians. The nadir of ethnic hostilities between Italians and the Québécois occurred in the 1990s when Parizeau, the leader of the provincial government attributed the loss of the separatist referendum to the ethnic vote, a codeword for Italians. In the mainstream press, Italian men were regularly depicted as violent criminals with connections to the Mafia, and Italian immigrant women were made fun of for being "fat black-clad mamas" (Miccone, 2012) in widow's garb, whose lack of formal education and language proficiency were seen as markers of their inferiority. The older Italian immigrant non-nas, who tended mini-vegetable gardens on balcony apartments, "picked chicory and dandelions from public parks" (Bonar, 1996) and gathered with female relatives to communally peel bushels of tomatoes for making tomato preserves, were seen as cultural throwbacks, peasants who lacked the civility or urban sophistication of city life. The religious beliefs and folk practices (e.g., religious shrines to saints on front lawns, Day of Dead rituals, belief in the evil eye) of many Italian immigrant women were seen as emblematic of Italians' lack of progress. The sense of inadequacy and inalienable other-ness that many Italian immigrant women and men were made to feel and still feel today, despite the class mobility they achieved, is a direct outcome of the discrimination they suffered. Italians who accumulated the wealth of the middle-class but none of the status and validation because the work they per-form (e.g., garment industry, janitorial work, home-sewing business, hospital porters, construction, welding, pipe fitting) does not carry the same dignity as other occupations embody what Richard Sennett and Jonathan Cobb referred to as the "hidden injuries of class."

Looking at the world through the lens of intersectionality, we come to see how different categories of identity and social status overlap and shape the experiences of historically marginalized groups. An older, working-class, immigrant woman Nonna Maria is disadvantaged along multiple axes—age, class, immigration status, and gender. But Nonna Maria's experiences do not fit neatly into simplistic models of male domination and female submission. She is more than a balance sheet of the ways in which she has been oppressed. Having been socialized to care for her family, Nonna cooks, cleans, and dotes on her grandson, even doing his laundry while her worry-free husband spends his time relaxing. She is still responsible for performing household chores. Indeed, Nonna spends the better part of her time worrying about the safety and welfare of her grandson, fussing about whether he has dressed appro-priately for the weather or eaten a home-cooked meal. In contrast, Luigi is often seen watching TV, unaware of the goings-on around him, while Nonna flutters around the house with boundless energy. Maria is constantly looking for ways to be occupied and stimulated, chatting with her grandson and getting him to tag along and chronicle her daily misadventures: visiting a flesh-and-blood Nonna in her own cantina or doing *la spesa* (grocery shopping), a site that is filled with all manner of entertainment (*Nonna Maria's TV,* 2012). If Nonna is filled with excitement and curiosity about the world, Luigi is content to stay home and passively follow her lead. Indeed, in the episode in which Nonna sees headline news warning about the sudden drop in temperature, she discovers that David has gone out without his jacket (Nonna Maria's TV, 2014). Accompanied by sound effects straight out of a Hitchcock thriller, the panic-stricken Nonna convinces her husband to help track down David, so that she can give him his jacket and feel at ease knowing that he will be properly attired. In the face of Nonna's dogged determination, Chef Luigi does not stand a chance and reluctantly agrees to drive her to the restaurant.

Indeed, aging Nonna is as persuasive as she is argumentative, an indomitable force of nature, which neither David nor Luigi can ever hope to match. Even though this older woman is responsible for the upkeep of the home, she resists being domesticated; she not only is an instigator of fun and mayhem but a resourceful immigrant woman who is unafraid to stand her ground and play by her own rules. She knows her mind and satisfies her desire for adventure with gusto and *joie de vivre*, finding pleasure in even the smallest everyday activities. While she provides David with a sense of security and warmth and performs her wifely duties admirably, she is not defined or cowed by the men in her life. Her enthusiasm remains steadfast, despite the challenges of immigration and the larger structures of oppression that have made her life difficult. In *Nonna's Maria Cantina Canadese*, Nonna refuses to be judged by her know-it-all grandson or her snobby relatives who think that she is not the genuine article. From the affluent, industrialized North, which blamed southern Italy for the country's social ills, to the federal government which labeled Italians as "nonpreferred immigrants" because they were considered backward, to the separatist Parti Québécoi (Quebec Party), who accused Italians of siding with the English establishment and causing the defeat of the 1995 referendum on national sovereignty for Quebec, Nonna lives in a world of powerful institutions that line up against her. Nevertheless, she is unafraid to be herself, to speak her hybrid language, and to take pride in her huge online following of diasporic Italians, a following which extends from Montreal to Sydney and beyond. Indeed, when the well-known Australian-Italian comic Joe Avati called Nonna for a chat, she was overjoyed. To her fans, Nonna has managed to overcome all manner of adversities: she survived war, migration, discrimination, and economic exploitation with her spirit intact. The anger and argumentativeness that Nonna expresses throughout the series could be interpreted as a form of sublimated hostility against those who have sought to exclude her. On a deeper level, though, her combativeness reveals a lack of belonging, a sense of being neither fully Canadian nor fully Italian, condemned to inhabiting a borderland of identity. The language policies of the separatist Quebec regime, which sought to distinguish "dyed-in-the-wool" Quebecers from those native Montrealers whose parents were not born in the province, has only helped to exacerbate the alienation that some Italian-Canadians feel toward both Francophone and Anglophone Quebec.

Of course, I have come to understand this context through my own experiences. I was raised in St. Michel, a working-class neighborhood where Italians and Francophones Quebecers lived side-by-side but often existed in parallel worlds. The Anglophones I met in university came from the deep suburbs I seldom visited, and when my brother bought a house in the English-speaking, upper-middle-class Town of Mount Royal, he may as well have moved to another country. As a second-generation ethnic academic who has written about older Italian immigrant women, many of whom were *nonnas*, the sense of chronic otherness that I felt in my youth (and continue to experience) motivated me to become an ethnographer. Like the French-Canadians who were told to "speak white," a slur that xenophobic Anglophones used against the speech of both Francophones and working-class people of color who hadn't mastered elite English, I too learned to speak the language of power and was rebuked when my speech betrayed my working-class, ethnic origins or expressed my discontent in ways that were considered too ethnic for my liberal arts colleagues in the United States. The university where I currently teach is unionized, and among my feminist colleagues in the Department of Gender Studies, there is no such pretense of cool detachment. We are not afraid to point out that female academics continue to bear the brunt of childcare and domestic work, while our male colleagues often shirk their responsibilities and forward their research agendas. We make the full range of our experiences known without fear of being judged weak or incompetent at our jobs for doing so. In Anthony Imperioli's loving parody of the older working-class Italian immigrant, Nonna refuses to "go gently into that good night." Watching *Nonna Maria's Cantina Canadese*, Italian ethnics such as me are invited to make ourselves vulnerable, to reflect on our experiences and own them in all of their complexity, all the while laughing and enjoying the difference that has made us who we are.

REFERENCES

Bonar, R. (1996). New perspectives on aged Italian women: Implications for minority groups of aged ethnic women. *Canadian Ethnic Studies, 28*(2), 64–81.

Del Negro, G. (2004). *Looking through my mother's eyes: Life stories of nine Italian immigrant women in Canada* (Second Edition). Guernica.

Iacovetta, F. (1993). *Such hardworking people: Italian immigrants in post-war Toronto* (Eleventh Revised Edition). McGill-Queens University Press.

Levinas, E. (1969). *Totality and infinity: An essay on exteriority.* (A. Lingis Trans.). Dusquene. (Original work published 1961).

Pizzi, N. (1957). Casetta in Canada [Song]. *Casetta in Canada.* RCA Italiana.

Ramirez, B. (1989). *Italians in Canada.* Canadian Historical Association.

Sennett, R. & J. Cobb. (1972). *The hidden injuries of class.* Alfred A. Knopf, Inc.

Nonna Maria's TV. (2009, March 7). *Nonna Maria and the Poutine* [Video file]. Retrieved from https://www.youtube.com/watch?v=-mJ6jczpS5k

Nonna Maria's TV. (2009, March 14). *Nonna Maria and Super Mario galaxy* [Video file]. Retrieved from https://www.youtube.com/watch?v=EZZVVLzvk3I

Nonna Maria's TV. (2009, May 19). *Nonna Maria's Cantina Canadese* [Video file]. Retrieved from https://www.youtube.com/watch?v=zGHyu1hTE2E

Nonna Maria's TV. (2010, October 28). *Nonna Maria's day at the salon* [Video file]. Retrieved from https://www.youtube.com/watch?v=OXD4cR1AZ5c

Nonna Maria's TV. (2011, January 30). *Nonna Maria's DVD disastro!* [Video file]. Retrieved from https://www.youtube.com/watch?v=syerM_ez_vc

Nonna Maria's TV. (2011, June 12). *Where's Nonna Maria?* [Video file]. Retrieved from https://www.youtube.com/watch?v=o4PGs5RGVUA

Nonna Maria's TV. (2012, February 12). *Nonna Maria Does La Spesa* [Video file]. Retrieved from https://www.youtube.com/watch?v=lXfyRbXNu1Y

Miccone, M. (2012, November 25). *Opinion: A long history of prejudice.* Montreal Gazette. https://montrealgazette.com/news/montreal/a-long-history-of-prejudice

Nonna Maria's TV. (2014, March 27). *Nonna Maria & Friends in: 15 Degrees or Mettere la Giacca Perché 'Sta Sera Fa Freddo!* [Video file]. Retrieved from https ://www.youtube.com/watch?v=h5fBaG0022k

Mastracci, D. (2018, July 14). *As a proud Italian-Canadian, I won't stand by my community's racism.* Huffington Post-Canada. https://www.huffingtonpost.ca/davide -mastracci/italian-canadian-immigrant-racism-mangiacake_a_23476352

Chapter 2

The Intersection of Race and Sexuality in Howard Cruse's *Stuck Rubber Baby*

Robert Kellerman

If we accept John Preston's observation that the best queer novels take place in the times and locations where people actually live,[1] then Howard Cruse's graphic novel *Stuck Rubber Baby* (Paradox Press, 1995; reissued Vertigo, 2010) would certainly rank as one of the best queer novels of the past 30 years. Its setting in the American South during the 1960s civil rights era allows Cruse to subtly examine the complex intersection of sexuality, race, and class among the sizeable cast of characters that populate the narrative.

One might argue, as some critics do, that the characters in the novel not only demonstrate these intersections but that the novel itself does as well. Julie Bickner Armstrong argues that the novel is a "work of movement fiction—where civil rights, usually coded as black, meets gay rights, mistakenly conceived of as white. Through those intersections the book creates a path where people and places from the margins move to center stage" (2018, p. 107); Gary Richards, reading the novel in terms of its genre, argues that it fuses the "white southern racial conversion narrative" with the "coming-out novel" (2012, p. 148).

Fusing these two movements and genres together allows for the intersectionality in the novel and the negotiation of the multiple identities that Cruse's characters have. How easily or not that characters negotiate identities differs radically based on their race and class. In some respects, the black queer characters move more freely through the novel than do the white queer characters, complicating the assertion made by the founder of the intersectionality theory Kimberlé Crenshaw "that if you're standing in the path of multiple forms of exclusion, you are likely to get hit by both" (2004, as cited in Meer, 2014). While that may be, in this novel the black characters are in some ways hit less hard than white characters.[2] This is perhaps unexpected, given that the white characters are alleged to be part of the power structure of the small town where the novel takes place, even if their inclusion in that structure varies widely. Thus, it becomes important to not only examine the characters but also the social and historical context in which the novel takes place, which has been justly praised for its specificity and historical veracity.[3]

Reading a text in context would seem to be a given, but it is not necessarily so in intersectionality theory (at least in its first iterations), which did not emerge as a specifically *literary* theory. Intersectionality as a construct for thinking about multiple identities "to focus attention on the vexed dynamics of difference and the solidarities of sameness in the context of antidiscrimination and social movement politics," as Cho, Crenshaw, and McCall put it (2013, p. 787), was first proposed in the legal field by Crenshaw in 1989. It has been adopted widely in the social sciences as a research methodology, where a great deal of intersectionality research has taken place. In its 30-year existence, social scientists have come to apply the theory in three different models. The first is the "additive" model, in which the various oppressions affecting a given individual are analyzed individually and believed to operate independently. As Mike C. Parent, Cirleen DeBlaere, and Bonnie Moradi put it, "Additive perspectives reflect the notion that minority identity statuses (e.g., race and gender) act independently and combine additively to shape people's experiences" (2013, p. 640). A black lesbian, for example, may well experience oppression for being black and for being a lesbian, but she would experience those oppressions separately. More subtle, perhaps, is the second, "multiplicative" or "interactionist" model, in which the various oppressions are experienced in relationship to and are influenced by each other; this model suggests that "beyond their independent effects, minority statuses and related experience may interact to shape people's experiences, with the typical implied nature of the interaction being that one minority status may exacerbate the effect of another" (Parent et al., 2013, p. 640). For example, the black lesbian's experience of oppression as a lesbian may be influenced by the fact that she is also black (and vice versa as well); she may be treated differently, than, say, a black gay man or a white lesbian. In simple terms, oppressions should not be viewed in isolation from each other (though they can be) but rather in integration with how they affect each other.

More recently, a third "intersectionist" model has emerged that seeks to explore that integration even more fully, maintaining that "multiple identities construct novel experiences that are distinctive and not necessarily divisible into their component parts" (Parent et al., 2013, p. 640); the experience of various oppressions is entirely integrated, in other words, and cannot be separated into analysis of any given oppression. If a person's experience of oppression is so individualized, then, that generalizing analysis becomes difficult, a logically progressive line of inquiry might be to analyze instead not the experience of a particular oppression or oppressions but rather the underlying societal structures that enable those oppressions. As Warner and Shields put it,

> While the individual experiences intersections as a coherent, individual social identity, intersections also reflect a complex operation of power relationships among social groups. In other words, there are different 'registers' of intersectionality, from personal experience to socio-structural dimension. . . . At its core, intersectionality is the embodiment in theory of the real-world fact that systems of inequality, from the experiential to the structural, are interdependent.

and that they should be studied in their entirety (2013, pp. 803-04). This shift in focus from an individual's experiences to the social structures that produce them—"the way things work rather than who people are," as Chun, Lipsitz, and Shin (2013, cited in Cho et al., 2013, p. 797) put it—reflects a growing understanding in the social sciences that researching subjects' experiences does not tell the whole story about how any given oppression works. Examining the entire system in which the oppression exists—what gives rise to it and how in turn its affects those under its influence—gives us more nuanced, complete analysis.

This is perhaps where *literary* analysis can best join the conversation. The human subjects of social science research may well experience common oppressions, but their individual lives may be so radically different from each other in experiencing oppressions that there may be no way to extrapolate any kind of commonalities among them, no way to situate their oppressions in a larger societal context. (For example, an upper-class, established, Latinx male may well experience queer oppression very differently from a recent, politically disenfranchised Latinx immigrant, so that analysis of the root system of oppression may not be consistent across individuals.) But because a literary text is always situated in a specific time and place, literary analysis can explore the setting of the text, its effects on the various characters inhabiting the text as the author presents them, or both, suggesting most closely the intersectionist model. Using intersectionality to examine a literary text has the potential to reveal the relationship between the microcosm of a character's particular situation and the macrocosm of the situation itself that is manifested in that character's experience. In a different context, Alison Bechdel expresses this idea directly in her introduction to the novel: "*Stuck Rubber Baby* is a story, but it's also a history—or perhaps more accurately a story about how history happens, one person at a time" (2010). The microcosm (or, rather, countless microcosms) is affected by and creates change to the macrocosm.

As Bechdel observes, this is precisely what *Stuck Rubber Baby* does. The novel presents an unusually wide range of characters in the fictional college town of Clayfield, Alabama—black, white, gay, lesbian, straight, well-off, and not so well-off—all of whom are dealing with the racial violence that rocked the American South in the 1960s. It tells the story from the point of view of Toland Polk, a well-meaning, young white man. Though the novel is essentially his story, his is not the only story: readers also see the effects of the social structure in Clayfield on that entire range of characters.

The first, most prominent intersection in the novel is that of sexuality and race, and Cruse complicates this intersection a great deal. One might expect the blacks in the novel to be doubly oppressed in the way that Crawford elucidates. In fact, they do not seem to be. While racial segregation drives the brutality against African Americans in Clayfield, the novel gives no evidence that it drives violence against the *queer* African Americans. In fact, nearly all the violence in the novel aimed at queer characters is aimed specifically at queer *white* characters. This may have simply been a choice on Cruse's part to keep the scope of the novel manageable, for a novel dealing with racial civil rights and queer visibility already has plenty on its narrative plate. But it might also suggest that for Clayfield's white power structure, queer African Americans are essentially invisible; as long as they can be kept in their place as black, then they will be kept in their place as queer as well, so that their queerness is irrelevant.

That said, it is how Clayfield's black community treats its queer members that commands interest. In general, it does so positively, and critics divide on this issue. There is certainly truth to the fact that many black communities (and especially black religious communities) can be highly homophobic, and Gary Richards takes the novel to task for this, noting that Cruse removes any aspect of black homophobia from it, writing that the novel misrepresents the complex stances that Southern African Americans took toward homosexuality (pp. 154, 162). But it is also true that black communities can be strongly supportive of their queer brothers and sisters, and that assuming that black communities are simply homophobic (particularly in the South) is also a distortion, as Simon Dickel notes. Citing E. Patrick Johnson's collection of oral histories from Southern black men, *Sweet Tea: Black Gay Men of the South* (2008, University of North Carolina Press) he argues that Johnson reminds us that the myth that the South is more repressive and backward in its attitudes toward gay men is counteracted by the many stories that he collected that suggest a more complex reality (Dickel, p. 618).

There is truth to both sides, of course—a region as complex as the American South can be both queer-negative *and* queer-positive simultaneously—but Cruse's choice to limit himself to presenting a supportive black community may be simply to keep the novel's scope manageable, as suggested above. Regardless of the choice, the queer black characters in the novel are valued, sometimes even beloved members of their community. For example, Esmo, a drag queen, performs regularly as Esmereldus at the AlleySax, a mixed bar on the outskirts of Clayfield, and is celebrated for his flamboyance. The bar is run by a lesbian couple, Marge and Effie, and they provide Clayfield with an alternative to the conservative power structure that runs the city. Queers dance together at the AlleySax, visiting jazz musicians regularly play there, and blacks and whites socialize together, especially during the bar's after hours—all activities that range from moderately to seriously radical in a small Southern town. (It is also notable that the other mixed-race establishment in town is the gay bar, the Rhombus.)

Perhaps the most interesting of the queer black characters is Les Pepper, the son of the Reverend Harland Pepper, the minister of Clayfield's influential, black Baptist church; and Anna Dellyne Pepper, his wife and former jazz singer who gave up her career to settle down in Clayfield. Les is openly gay and, more importantly, sexually active; he has not been "neutered" to make him more palatable. In fact, Toland's first sexual experience with a man is with Les, in a hotel where Les nonchalantly maintains a stash of clothing to change into in the morning for whenever he has an overnight sexual encounter. He is forthright when Toland asks him if his parents know that he's gay, saying, "*Mama* knows. It's cool. She's *always* had *'sissy friends.'* An' Papa knows.—Which ain't to say he's ever said the first *word* about knowing" (Cruse, 1995, p. 47).[4] As someone who worked as a jazz singer, it is not surprising that Anna Dellyne knew queer people, and the Reverend Pepper maintains a "don't ask, don't tell" stance that is not uncommon among families for whom a queer member could be considered a liability. But Les actually is an asset, someone whom his parents, particularly his father, depend on when the movement demands it. Following a bombing at the hotel, the Reverend Pepper appears at the Rhombus, Clayfield's gay bar, to fetch him and help organize a response. Toland notes that "*Les* stayed at his Daddy's *beck* and *call.* I was *impressed* at how a *partyboy* from the *Rhombus* could turn into a perfect *preacher's kid* at the flick of a *switch*" (Cruse, 1995, p. 106).

He also provides the implicit, unstated connection between the racial civil rights movement and the queer civil rights movement that would come later in American history (though of course many elements of the novel do that—the gathering spaces just mentioned, for example). On first meeting Toland at the Rhombus, Les says that after his father stopped pressuring him to get married, "Martin Luther King *himself* could walk up an' say to me, 'Les, you gotta *quit* bein' *gay!'* . . . An' I'd say to him, "*Sure thing,* Dr. King—just as soon as *you* stop bein' *Negro!*" (Cruse, 1995, p. 48). His understanding that his identities are immutable does not necessarily mean that he experiences intersectionality in an integrative way. It seems more that he has compartmentalized his queerness and his blackness so that one does not impinge on the other, at least with his father, as he does in the incident noted earlier—though it is also worth noting, however, his gayness seems to be a nonissue elsewhere in the black community, where he is gay *and* black rather than gay *or* black.

The queer African Americans in Clayfield, then, carve out a safe space for themselves by making themselves valuable to the subcommunity to which they belong. The community in turn values them for their contributions to the civil rights cause: providing a safe space, showing up at demonstrations, being part of church communities, being at the beck and call of the preacher who leads the nonviolent protests, all actions which are documented in the novel. Their placement in the larger context of the Clayfield power structure contrasts sharply with that of Toland, who, at least initially, seems to belong to no particular community.

In general, Toland's relationships to others are tenuous. His parents are killed in an automobile accident early in the novel, and his one sister Melanie is married to a white supremacist, Orley, who opposes integration and Toland's slow (and reluctant) involvement in the black community protests. Nor did his upbringing give him a broad-minded view of the world; as Bechdel notes, Toland is the

> archetypal nice person. A white southerner who grew up steeped in the casual as well as institutional racism of Jim Crow, he wouldn't intentionally hurt anyone—but then again, he doesn't intentionally do much of anything at all. He's drifting along, equally disengaged from himself and the world. (2010)

His parents, though kind and well meaning, have the prejudices that so many other white Southerners who had no particular investment in the civil rights movement had. His father, for example, gives Stetson, the black man he employs as a handyman, grudging respect. When a young Toland asks him if there is a difference between the skulls of white people and black people, his father suggests that black skulls are probably stronger because black people are "closer to the animal state," and continues, "Now as far as *brains* are concerned, it's another matter. White people's brains are more *developed* [than black brains]. It's been scientifically proven." Immediately after, he warns, "Don't ever make the mistake of failin' to *respect* the *colored man,* son. Treated well, he'll do *better* by you than many a *white*" (Cruse, 1995, pp. 2-3). Likewise, his mother forces the younger Toland to take a shower after he exchanges clothes with Stetson's son as part of a game, though to his credit even a young Toland wonders why this is necessary. And though his father owned a sizeable library, his sister points out to him after their parents' death in a car accident, "Don't *tell* me that you thought Daddy had actually *read* all of these books!" (Cruse, 1995, p. 3).

Furthermore, Toland is as uneducated as his parents, aimlessly treading water in Clayfield by working a modest job in a gas station. Many of the other white characters with whom he is acquainted are distanced from him because not only they are politically aware and sympathetic to the civil rights cause but also because they have a wider view of the world. For example, Ginger Raines, his erstwhile girlfriend with whom he takes up a relationship to prove his heterosexuality (and with whom he fathers a child, the "stuck rubber baby" of the title), is a music student at the local, presumably private college in Clayfield, where her father is on the board of trustees. She is from Akron, Ohio, and thus an outsider—a clear example of a character based on the Northern white sympathizers who came South to join the protests and work in the movement. She spends more time involved in the civil rights movement than she does on her schoolwork. When she is suspended from school and is only reinstated because her father has some clout and on the condition that she not be involved in any civil right organizations, she freely admits that she will continue to be involved in the local Equality League, only in a more circumspect way. This is the focus of her life at this point, and it is assumed that she will not stay in Clayfield but will move on to her music career, which she does, as we see in a brief episode late in the novel.

Likewise, Riley Wheeler, a local boy with whom Toland shares a house, has been in the military and seen some of the world. While not as strongly sympathetic to the civil rights movement, he and his girlfriend Mavis befriend Toland, Ginger, and Sammy Noone, the other major gay white character in the novel, who eventually also moves into the house. (It so happens that Riley and Mavis moved in together while they were still in high school and so as a couple defy the norms of conservative Clayfield.) In all these cases, education or travel—seeing more of the world than Clayfield—distances them from Toland.

Like Riley, Sammy Noone is also a military veteran and the organist at the politically progressive Episcopal church in Clayfield. In contrast to Toland, Sammy has some social standing because of his talent and education (he teaches music as a sideline), and he is further contrasted in that he is openly gay. As someone who is more public both in social standing and in his sexuality, Sammy is more of a threat to the heterosexual power structure in town, though clearly any queer in Clayfield, regardless of social standing, is a target for violence. At the beginning of the novel, Toland reports for the draft and checks the box "homosexual" on his medical history questionnaire, thus avoiding the draft and establishing that he is well aware that he is gay, but he recalls Ezra Gable, the president of Clayfield's biggest bank, who was murdered by teenagers allegedly for being gay, and Abby Baxter, the presumably lesbian school nurse who is the target of social ridicule and decides that "this *homo* stuff had to get nipped *right* in the *bud!*" (Cruse, 1995, p. 10).

Regardless of social class, all queers in Clayfield live in fear, on the margins, or both. So too with Sammy. His wealthy family has disowned him because of his homosexuality despite the honor of his military service, so that he must scrounge for a living and at one point return home to beg that his father help support him. Though there are deaths in the novel, Sammy's is the one brutal death that we witness in detail as readers. In the circumstances of Sammy's lynching at the hands of white supremacists, Cruse again draws the parallels between the violence waged against African Americans and queers. Sammy becomes notorious in the pages of the white supremacist newspaper *The Dixie Patriot* with the headline "Pervert on Payroll of Race-Mixing Church," to the point that where its normally sympathetic, liberal rector, the Reverend Edgar Morris, demands that he leave both his apartment on the church property and his organist position. He justifies his demands by stating that "Trinity Episcopal is already a *target* because of the position I've taken on integration. The race baiters will make *hash* of me if I'm seen as condoning *homosexuality*" (Cruse, 1995). Sammy's lynching is the key to Toland's public coming out, but to get to that point, his struggle to acknowledge that he is gay is long and difficult.

Much is made of Toland's status as a bystander to many of the events of the novel and his emotional detachment from them. He is not nearly as involved and passionate about civil rights as he feels he ought to be, even as events of the movement—lynchings, beatings, passive resistance sit-ins, as well as the real-life 1964 March on Washington—unfold around him. When asked by his girlfriend Ginger Raines whether he is feeling that he is where he ought to be as they are attending the March on Washington, he does not answer her directly. Instead, he thinks:

> Her question caught me *short* because the fact was, I *hadn't* felt that way. I'd pretty much *always* felt like an inadequate *bozo* stuck in the *wrong* place, doing the *wrong* thing nine-tenths of the time. But maybe not *this* time, I thought, looking around me. The fact was, being there in Washington that particular day could *pass* for the feeling of rightness that Ginger was *talking* to me about. (Cruse, 1995, p. 103)

And when the Melody Motel, where the black community organizes its protests, is bombed, Toland wanders around while many of his friends are trying to help, unsure of his place in this community: "I started getting *depressed* over how out of *place* I felt. And when I considered how damn *typical* it was of me to go into a funk over my own disconnectedness when other people's *children* were *dead* or bleeding . . . it made me even *more* depressed!" (Cruse, 1995, p. 107).

But Toland is jerked into reality after Sammy's lynching. He correctly feels that he is partly responsible for his death, as he was with Sammy at the place they share with Riley and Mavis (who moved in after he lost his church job), got drunk with him, fended off his sexual advances but allowed Sammy to go to the offices of the *Dixie Patriot* and declare himself the "pervert" at the "race-mixing church." White supremacists show up late at night, knock out Toland cold, and lynch Sammy, who is killed for being gay *and* for being sympathetic to the black civil rights movement. This lynching finally makes clear to Toland exactly what is at stake for him personally. When he is dealing with the police following the murder, they inform him, "Let's just say we *know* what you *are*" and advise him to stay on the right side of the law (Cruse, 1995, p. 183), and he knows that he too is a target.

The novel's climax occurs at Sammy's memorial service at the AlleySax. When Toland takes the stage to speak, he cries uncontrollably and tells the reader that he cannot remember any of the words he had spoken except for four:

> "It could've been *me*." He continues, "And I *realized* as I *spoke* those four words that I was saying them to *Shiloh* [the leader of the black choir the Freedom Singers, who was seriously injured in the hotel bombing] more than to anyone *else*. I knew I'd find *understanding* in Shiloh's *eyes*. (Cruse, 1995, p. 193)

In coming to realize that as a gay man he is as much a target for violence as are Clayfield's black citizens, the novel's two concerns—the civil rights movement and Toland's coming-out story—are inextricably woven together.

Richards argues that in the novel the black characters are problematic in that their primary function as an entire community is to help Toland come out, so that "virtually every black character . . . gains his or her most lasting stature within the novel through the mentoring of the white gay Toland Polk" (2012, p. 167-168), and in so doing fills the role of subservient blacks to the whites. In many cases it is true that the black characters do collectively contribute to Toland's coming out; Les in Toland's first sexual experience comes to mind. In another notable scene, Les's mother Anna Dellyne has a conversation with Toland when he has offered to marry Ginger, whom he has gotten pregnant. She tells him the story of a gay jazz musician she worked with who entered a disastrous marriage which predictably fell apart, and everybody lost all respect for him. She concludes by saying, "Not that *you'd* be ludicrous playin' straight, sugar! There's not a *doubt* in my *mind* you'd pull it off better than *Shelby* did! Still, I'd *think* a little more about it if I was you, about tryin' to be what you're *not*" (Cruse, 1995, p. 133).

But it is notable that many other events also contribute to his coming out—his discussion with Ginger about being gay, his visits to both the Rhombus and the Alleysax, and especially his interactions with Sammy. Sammy's death in particular is the impetus for Toland's coming out declaration at the memorial service. His statement "It could've been me" encapsulates the microcosm, the personal decision to publicly come out, which is set in the macrocosm of the novel's setting, and it heightens the intersections between the two.

Dickel notes that the two oppressions in the novel—racism and homophobia—are clearly related but not analogous. Though coming out can be fraught with fear and even danger for any queer person, the inclusion of black characters for whom being out is not problematic for them or for their community strongly contrasts them with Toland (2011, p. 630). To be fair, we do not witness the coming out story of any of the black characters, and when Toland comes out to some characters—Ginger and his sister Melanie, for example—he is not rejected. However, they are not analogous, in that coming out as a public act is a choice in a way that being black is not, and for Toland to come out more fully, he must also choose to leave Clayfield—a decision that many queer people took to migrate to larger, more tolerant, often urban areas, and to find a community that queer people in Clayfield lack and the black community has (and to which its queer members belong).

If he previously had no education or view of the wider world, Toland acquires it upon leaving, although we as readers see only brief glimpses of his life trajectory after Clayfield. There is a brief episode in San Francisco late in the novel set in the late 1960s, where Toland has joined the counterculture and become a hippie. There he meets his former brother-in-law Orley, also now a hippie, whom Melanie threw out and divorced after he confessed to her—and confesses to Toland in their brief meeting—that he let the *Dixie Patriot* know that Sammy was a "*race-mixer*" and "*queer* as a *three-dollar bill*." With this confession, Orley in effect contributed to Sammy's murder, if he was not directly responsible. After Orley begs for forgiveness, Toland tells him, "I *loved* Sammy. He was a good *friend* and he made me *braver* than I would've been *otherwise*" (Cruse 1995, p. 198). His self-knowledge of his gayness by this time extends to his own implication in Sammy's lynching: after all, if he had not rebuffed Sammy's sexual advances, then Sammy would not have gone out that night.

The other glimpses of Toland's current life frame the novel in its opening and closing and are interspersed throughout, so that the entire novel is in fact told in flashback. We learn that a now middle-aged Toland is living with a partner in a presumably Northern city (as the scene is set in winter). Dickel notes the important detail of the "Silence=Death" ACT UP poster in a panel late in the novel (2011, p. 631), and his partner, though not part of the narrative per se, occasionally consoles the present-day Toland as he tells the most emotionally painful parts of the story. Clearly, Toland has found an activist community and a relationship, though we do not know how he got to that place. We only know that he has gotten there.

One of the major themes of the novel is how related the black civil rights movement was to the queer rights movement. Tony Kushner puts it best in his introduction to the original edition of the novel: "It [the novel] articulates a crying need for solidarity; it performs the crucial function of remembering, for the queer community, how essential to the birth of our politics of liberation the civil rights movement was" (1995, p. iv). Solidarity—in the context of the novel, community—is what makes the intersection of the race and sexuality nonproblematic for the queer African Americans, and a lack of solidarity with any community is what makes the intersection of social class and sexuality impossible for Toland—at least as long as he stays in Clayfield. The novel thus retells the story that poses the questions every queer person must answer in his or her specific place and time: How do I come out? What happens when I do? As it happens, these are the same questions that an intersectional approach asks: Where do I fit in? How do I fit in?

NOTES

1. Preston makes this point in his introduction to *Domesticity Isn't Pretty*, the first collection of Tim Barela's serial comic strip *Leonard and Larry* (1993). He writes:

I've never really understood why, but somehow it seems that many people are convinced that a narrative set in St. Paul's or on the shores of Fire Island somehow becomes more *important*. I think this is a strange and self-defeating deception. The best stories are set in the place where they happen. (p. 7)

2. I have chosen the term "black" rather than "African American" throughout the essay. This term is consistent with that used in the novel itself and in most of the criticism of the novel.

3. For example, Buckner notes that the events of the novel that take place in the fictional Clayfield—demonstrations in a city park, the bombing of the motel where protest activities are coordinated, and so on—mirror those that historically took place in Birmingham, Alabama (p. 107). Dickel notes that the mix of real 1960s song lyrics with those that Cruse wrote for specific characters grounds the novel in real life as well (p. 620).

4. To render the dialogue in a graphic novel (or, for that matter, a comic strip) accurately poses a puzzle. As do many cartoonists and graphic novelists, Cruse writes his dialogue entirely in upper-case lettering, with emphases rendered in boldface. I have chosen to "translate" this into the more conventional typesetting mix of upper- and lower-case lettering, and to render his boldface emphases in *italics*.

REFERENCES

Armstrong, J. B. (2018). Stuck Rubber Baby and the intersection of civil rights historical memory. In M. J. Cutter and C. J. Schlund-Vials (Eds.), *Redrawing the historical past: History, memory, and multiethnic graphic novels.* University of Georgia Press.

Bechdel, A. (2010). Foreword. In H. Cruse (Ed.), *Stuck rubber baby.* Paradox Press.

Cho, S., Crenshaw, K. W., and McCall, L. Toward a field of intersectionality studies: Theory, applications, and praxis. *Signs, 38*(4), 785–810.

Cruse, H. (1995). *Stuck rubber baby.* Vertigo.

Dickel, S. (2011). "Can't leave me behind": Racism, gay politics, and coming of age in Howard Cruse's *Stuck Rubber Baby. Amerikastudien/American Studies, 56*(4), 617–635.

Kushner, T. (1995). Intro. In H. Cruse (Ed.), *Stuck rubber baby.* Vertigo.

Meer, N. (2014). *SAGE key concepts: Key concepts in race and ethnicity.* SAGE UK.

Parent, M., DeBlaere, C, and Morelli, B. (2013). Approaches to research on intersectionality: Perspectives on gender, LGBT, and racial/ethnic identities. *Sex Roles* (68), 639–645.

Preston, J. (1993). Foreword. In T. Barela (Ed.), *Domesticity isn't pretty.* Palliard Press.

Richards, G. (2012). Everybody's graphic protest novel: *Stuck Rubber Baby* and the anxieties of racial difference. In B. Costello and Q. J. Whitted (Eds.), *Comics and the U.S. South.* University Press of Mississippi.

Warner, L. R., & Shields, S. A. (2013). The intersection of sexuality, gender, and race: Identity research at the crossroads. *Sex Roles* (68), 803–810.

Chapter 3

A Work in Progress

Advancing Intersectionality in and through Queer Television

Katrina T. Webber and Layla Cameron

Sedgwick accurately claimed in 2004 that *The L Word* would "make a real and unpredictable difference in the overall landscape of the media world" (n.p.). Indeed, it was "the first show in television history to place recurring lesbian, genderqueer, and bisexual characters front and center" (Heller, 2014, p. 130). While certainly one of the most progressive shows of its time, *The L Word* (aired on Showtime between 2004 and 2009) has been heavily criticized for its portrayal of queer peoples' lives. Centering overwhelmingly on white, thin, and upper-class characters, both the cast and the storylines featured on the original series were certainly not reflective of its devoted audience; criticisms include its emphasis on monogamy, its adherence to heteronormative norms and ideals, its poor representation of trans communities, the erasure of disabled communities, a lack of body diversity, and the lack of masculine and androgynous queer female and nonbinary characters (Akass & McCabe, 2006; Burns & Davies, 2009; Cefai, 2014; Chawansky & Francombe, 2013; Guthrie et al, 2013). However, *The L Word* remains a hallmark for queer communities due to its rare use of insider reflexive knowledge and consequential ability to provide "specific pleasures" to those "in the know" (Moore, 2007, p. 5). Much to the series' devoted fans' delight, *The L Word* was granted a reboot in the form of *The L Word: Generation Q* (2019-ongoing, herein referred to as *Gen Q*). Featuring a handful of original cast members in addition to a roster of new actors, the reboot appears to address *some* of its predecessor's flaws. This is no easy feat, as making media about queer people in a realistic way is "a minefield of contradiction that can be construed as both disabling and empowering but is by no means easily representable" (Heller, 2014, p. 129). Nevertheless, *Gen Q* attempts to maintain an intersectional focus.

There was a lot of pressure on *Gen Q* to fulfill the desires of its dedicated fan base. Many viewers felt the significance of watching *The L Word* for the first time, particularly for the meaningful experience of seeing our communities—or what we desired to be our communities—played out on screen. Nostalgia involves an emotional response for the past and that which is no longer, highlighting the gap left by *The L Word* after it stopped airing in 2009 and the hunger that audiences felt. Padva (2014) argues that "[nostalgia] creates an emotional landscape, a sentimental environment that cherishes past experiences, whether these are personal or communal occurrences" (p. 3). This longing was obvious in the think pieces that came out in preparation for the reboot, which were both optimistic and critical of the original series (e.g., Webster, 2019), with many arguing that the reboot was a political deviation of its very sanitized predecessor (Gordon-Loebl, 2020; Hyndman, 2019). Importantly, focusing on the politics of the reboot is an essential practice that cannot be lost in favor of this nostalgia, as media representations of queer people "help people understand who they are and the challenges they can expect to face with regard to this particular identity" (Waggoner, 2018, p. 1880).

What do shows like *Gen Q* owe queer audiences? In response to criticisms of the original show, its creator Ilene Chaiken (who worked as executive producer on the reboot) was clear that she was not in the business of making ethical television, arguing further that such values were incompatible with the television industry (Heller, 2014). While Chaiken never claimed to be making socially responsible television (Glock, 2005), the significance of this program for queer viewers paired with the underrepresentation of queer people arguably posits that there is always an underlying sense of ethical responsibility to queer communities:

> Communitarian ethics is steeped in the ethical tradition of morality and sense of duty . . . the same facets of consequentialism (good outweighs the bad), duty (responsibility), and virtue (shaped by the person) still translate into narrative television, especially when it involves representation of the Other. (Waggoner, 2018, pp. 1880–1881)

Further, according to the USC Annenberg School for Communication and Journalism's Critical Media Project, "The media uses representations— images, words, and characters or personae—to convey specific ideas and values related to culture and identity in society" (n.d., "Key Concepts" para. 1). "Therefore, [media representations] are not neutral or objective. They are constructed and play an important role in imparting ideology" (n.d., "Key

Concepts" para. 5). Thus, this representation of Othered populations (or lack thereof) shapes not only how mainstream society understands and places value on certain identities but also how these Othered populations understand their own identity and perceived value on a mass scale. It is an understatement to say that values hold a great deal of power "because we internalize them and take them for granted . . . they can shape the way we see and understand the people, objects, practices, and institutions in our lives" (n.d., "Key Concepts" para. 3). Therefore, scholars such as Waggoner (2018) argue that writers and showrunners who have the authority to make decisions regarding plot and character development have a responsibility to viewers because such representations influence how viewers understand themselves and each other. Additionally, while these programs are educational sites for straight people about queer identities, relationships, and communities, "for lesbian communities, ethics has been less a question of individual moral value than a communitarian effort to shape values in 'lesbian contexts' than enable resistance to limitation and domination" (Heller, 2014, p. 126). *The L Word*, and arguably its successor, was successful precisely because of fan engagement and "a passionate sense of cultural ownership of its stories and characters" (Heller, 2014, p. 128).

While Chaiken worked to distance herself, and by extension, *The L Word*, from politics, the original program touched on many important political issues, including marriage equality, same-sex parenting/reproductive practices, addiction, foster care, Don't Ask Don't Tell military policies, and gender transition. These issues, or those similar, continue to impact queer communities today, and "the narratives that television shows present are the historical and institutional sites for these conversations and identities to be addressed" (Waggoner, 2018, p. 1878). Excitingly, as Gordon-Loebl (2020) writes, "It's clear, watching the reboot, that creator Ilene Chaiken and showrunner Marja-Lewis Ryan are making a concerted effort to rectify some of the missteps of the original series" (n.p.). Hyndman (2019) continues:

> The *Generation Q* spin feels far more focused on big, modern-day feminist and queer power moves than the raw fuck-up lesbian stories of the original—which begs the question: will the series take on a greater socio-political overtone vs focusing on the small-world realities lesbians face every day? (Hyndman, 2019, n.p.)

Set over 10 years after the original *The L Word* series, *Gen Q* is a sequel consisting of some original cast members, alongside many new faces centering LGBTQ+ characters' triumphs and tribulations when it comes to friendship, sex, love, family, careers, and personal growth. The show focuses on a few key plot points for original *L Word* cast members: Bette Porter (played by

Jennifer Beals) running for office while dealing with the backlash of a secret affair; Alice (Leisha Hailey) managing her successful talk show and relationship with Nat (Stephanie Allynne), while also navigating cordial relationships with Nat's ex-wife (Gigi, played by Sepideh Moafi) and children; Shane (Katherine Moennig) moving back to LA. The new generation cast members' experiences are focused on the following key plot points: Dani (Arienne Mandi) taking a job on Bette Porter's staff and her recent engagement to Sophie (Rosanny Zayas); Sophie working for Alice while dealing with Dani's always putting work or her father's expectations or wants above their relationship; Finley (Jacqueline Toboni) moving in with Shane, exploring a relationship with a minster, and shoving down a difficult past with alcohol; Micah (Leo Sheng) getting to know a crush, dabbling with hookup apps, and dealing with a mother who continues to refer to times before he transitioned.

Each episode of *Gen Q* was immediately followed by a new program, *Work in Progress*, which is a semi-autobiographical series about Abby (played by Abby McEnany), a self-identified "fat, queer dyke," who, after various mishaps and misfortunes in life and frustration with her own mental health, enters a surprising new relationship just a few days after committing to counting down the days until she will end her life. Abby's new love interest, Chris (Theo Germaine) is a 22-year-old trans man. Applying a "hermeneutic of feminist suspicion" (McFadden, 2010, p. 422), the authors conduct qualitative content analyses of both eight-episode seasons to assess representations of queer communities on *The L Word: Generation Q* and *Work in Progress*. These two series were chosen because they were both produced by and aired on Showtime, and newly premiered on December 8, 2019, one right after the other. Additionally, both series tackle taboo sociopolitical topics, while aiming to have a more diverse character and/or actor representation on screen. Utilizing an intersectional feminist approach grounded in critical race studies, disability studies, fat studies, and queer theory, the authors argue that *Work in Progress* adequately responds to the call for more diverse and complex representations on screen, whereas *The L Word: Generation Q*—while certainly more radical than its predecessor—falls flat in comparison.

Perhaps one of the most glaring omissions was the lack of body diversity in *Gen Q*. Considering the increasing mainstream popularity of body-positive rhetoric (Cwynar-Horta, 2016) and its roots in queer and lesbian activist efforts (Cooper, 2016), it was disappointing to see a thin body ideal maintained in the reboot. The original *L Word* contributes to the trope of fat people as undesirable, asexual, and unworthy of representation via symbolic annihilation (Gerbner & Gross, 1976; Giovanelli & Ostertag, 2009; Tuchman et al., 1978) of larger bodies on the program; the absence of fat lesbians prioritizes or values thin queer bodies. The quantity (frequency) and quality (non-stereotypical) representation of fat bodies in the media are few and far between as it is, so this omission is not surprising. Keeping fat bodies out of sight and out of mind serves to erase their existence (Gerbner & Gross, 1976; Gross, 1991; Tuchman et al., 1978) and deem those bodies asexual within the context of a show otherwise openly portraying queer and diverse identity and sexuality. Streitmatter (2009) points to news coverage of the original series, arguing that every piece touched on the conventional physical attractiveness of the show's characters. Similarly, *Gen Q* remains very focused on thin bodies. In Episode Seven, Micah's mother comments on how Micah looks like he lost weight, furthering the perpetuation of the thin/appearance ideal. Additionally, there are no actors in the show that fall outside of the traditionally thin/athletic bodies seen in media. The few exceptions are both small supporting roles, such as Heather, played by Fortune Feimster, who is the announcer for Alice's show.

There is much more body diversity in *Work in Progress*. Significantly, Abby self-identifies as fat. Within the first minute of the first episode, there is a shot of Abby reading *Shrill*, a popular memoir-turned TV series in part about fat activism written by Lindy West. Abby is not exactly proud to be fat. She complains of "feeling fat" to her sister, attends "Best Self" meetings that are replicas of Weight Watchers/WW meetings, and in Episode Seven enacts the trope of "ordering for a friend" at a donut shop so she can binge on coffee and donuts. However, much like *Shrill*, Abby embodies the mixed feelings many fat people can identify with, particularly negative feelings and a desire for weight loss that "bad fatties" may experience in response to structural or systemic instances of oppression and discrimination (Brown & Herndon, 2020). Importantly, Abby's feelings do not seem to take away from the overall fat-positive stance of the show, which McEnany explains is perhaps its most revolutionary aspect (Dry, 2020).

Although Abby's friends are predominantly white, there is a mix of gender expressions and body sizes. Abby is also introduced to body-positive queer spaces by Chris, her love interest. In Episode Two, while attending a "Best Self" meeting, Chris texts Abby to invite her to a nightclub where burlesque performers of different sizes and gender presentations serve as entertainers. In the next episode (Three), Abby calls out Weird Al Yankovic—Julia Sweeney's husband—for his offensive song "Fat'" Additionally, it is culturally significant that *Work in Progress* uses the word "fat" in its promotional materials to describe its main character. Of course, some "televisual trends . . . commercially exploit the perennial promise of newness in everything from reality programming to antidepressants and sexual identities" (Heller, 2014, p. 139). Even if this were the reasoning behind the efforts made by *Work in Progress*, it would have been encouraging to see such exploitation of body-positive rhetoric by *Gen Q*.

Consumerism and the spending power of lesbians remained a contentious topic among viewers of the original *L Word*. Many criticized the spending power and class status of its main characters as unrealistic (Guthrie et al, 2013). Continuing this erasure, most of the original cast featured on *Gen Q* have become significantly wealthier than they were during the original series, as Berman (2019) writes,

> With their glamorous jobs and rich-people problems, Bette, Alice, and Shane are living the same sparkly postfeminist fantasies that hooked viewers in the aughts. That leaves the more diverse *Generation Q* characters to represent the politically engaged, sexually fluid, and trans-inclusive present. (n.p.)

Indeed, Bette is running for mayor of Los Angeles and has upgraded to a larger home, Alice is an Ellen-esque host of a television show, and Shane nonchalantly moves into a mansion as she returns to Los Angeles—a home for which, over brunch in the first episode, Alice and Bette swiftly order a bed upon hearing that Shane has not fully furnished her home. *Gen Q* certainly evinces an upper-class air, despite the more realistic circumstances of the next generation. For example, Sophie and Dani face many difficulties navigating their class differences as they begin planning their wedding. Finley, who has no working car, alludes to not making much as Alice's personal assistant and crashes at Shane's oversized new home after mentioning she lives in a small apartment with several people.

Constructing a set featuring a home or domestic space offers an opportunity to explore issues about socioeconomic class. Cefai (2014) writes that the use of location in *The L Word* is critical to developing a show centered on a sexual minority. Creators Chaiken and Ryan use the urban sprawl of Los Angeles to build feelings of camaraderie, visibility, and acceptance and encourage the viewer to "think about the intentional mobilization of place as a trajectory of gay representation that shapes the visibility of feeling" (p. 653). The original series is based in West Hollywood, a queer-friendly, expensive neighborhood in Los Angeles. The cast of *Gen Q* is still located in Los Angeles, but this time in Silver Lake, a historically queer and ethnically diverse neighborhood known for its trendy cultural life in the forms of restaurants, bars, and clubs, but slightly more affordable. While both the significantly less wealthy next-generation characters on *Gen Q* and the characters on *Work in Progress* inhabit middle-class living spaces, *Work in Progress* utilizes those spaces in ways that feel much more intimate and allow for deeper character development. For example, the slow reveal over the course of the season of Abby's hall closet that holds boxes upon boxes of journals filled with notes from her manic and depressive episodes brings the viewer into the living space and utilizes physical space as a key storytelling figure.

Gender nonconforming, nonbinary, and trans folks were largely missing from *The L Word*; the original series relied heavily on a binary view of gender, with queer femme and masculine depictions drawing from heteronormative tropes. When trans folks were included, *The L Word* relied on problematic narratives regarding gender identity, with the featured trans character Max, maintaining that they were trapped inside the wrong body. Viewers reiterated these problematic depictions (Kern, 2012). Much discussion has occurred about the representations of trans people and gender-nonconforming people, an important fallout considering that "when a niche audience is 'baited' into watching a show because of a promise of positive representation, perhaps more conversation should be had regarding falling into clichéd tropes that have shown harm and discord in the past" (Waggoner, 2018, p. 1889). Excitingly, Ryan, the showrunner and an executive producer for *Gen Q*, announced that *Gen Q* was largely responding to TERF (trans-exclusionary radical feminist) lesbians (Topel, 2019). To achieve this, creators cast trans actors to play characters whose trans identity is not always central to the character, or in two instances (bartender Tess, played by Jamie Clayton, and Angie's love interest Jordi, played by Sophie Giannamore), were written as cisgendered. Furthermore, some of the characters, such as Finley, embody gender nonconforming behaviors and aesthetics, and at least one trans writer was hired (Gordon-Loebl, 2020). Lewis-Ryan also asserted that there was "somebody in almost every department who represents the trans and non-binary experience" (Walker, 2019, n.p.). However, gender nonconformity, nonbinary, or explicitly genderqueer characters are not identified or explored in meaningful depth.

In contrast, *Work in Progress* explicitly posed gender identity as central to the storyline, particularly through the character development of Chris, Abby's love interest. In the first episode, Abby reads Chris as a cis woman and lesbian, but he later corrects her that he identifies as a trans man. While already having identified herself as a lesbian, Abby immediately responds that she is still interested in going on a date, showing that gender is not a factor in desirability for Abby. The show continues to use Chris's gender identity to highlight trans issues, as Abby's friends and family continue to struggle with misgendering Chris. However, this is not done in a tokenizing way; as Abby states in Episode Two, "It is not the job of the queer community to teach the straight cis community" (5:50). Rather, this blunt approach to discussing gender allows informed and/or queer audiences a sense of relief and an opportunity to identify with the characters, while also calling-in cis viewers who may be new to conversations about gender identity and pronouns. An interesting example is the storyline surrounding Julia Sweeney's *Saturday Night Live* character, Pat, referred to by Julia's daughter as a "gender minstrel." In this narrative arc where Abby befriends Julia unexpectedly, Abby expresses how negatively this character affected her life due to their resemblance when she was younger, inviting Julia to be accountable for the harm this character

caused. The show has many blunt and forceful examples of gender nonconformity, such as a host of genderqueer characters within Chris' friend group
who, throughout the season, introduce Abby to new ways of thinking about
gender, relationships, family, and sexuality. In one scene, a friend of Chris'
sells handmade leather goods at a nightclub and excitedly tells Chris about
receiving a new form of identification, mentioning the abandonment of a
"deadname."[1]

Sexuality was, at times, a missed opportunity in *The L Word* to discuss
gender identity, queerness, ethical nonmonogamy, and sexual fluidity. Often
when bisexuality became a topic of conversation, many of the lesbian characters scoffed or appeared disgusted at the idea of engaging sexually with a
cis man; even trans characters or gender-nonconforming characters (such as
Kit's love interest, Ivan) were received with hesitation. In *Gen Q*, sexuality
and relationship structures appear to be more fluid, particularly through the
development of a "throuple" involving Alice, Nat, and Gigi, further explored
by Alice when she conducts an interview about polyamory with queer black
writer Roxane Gay. However, the interview ends with Nat proclaiming her
love for Alice—and only Alice—insinuating that the throuple was not sustainable long-term. Additionally, various characters (Sophie, Finley, and
Bette) become involved in affairs throughout the season, maintaining a criticism from the original series that queer women are portrayed as hypersexual
in ways that confront ethical boundaries.

However, sexuality remains a consistent and complex topic central to the
storyline of *Work in Progress*. The series does an excellent job of normalizing consensual sex, particularly through the intimate and explicit dialogue
between Chris and Abby leading up to their first sexual encounter in Episode
Three. The first time Abby and Chris have sex is messy, awkward, innocent,
and sweet. This is partly made possible because beforehand, while in a car-
share service (i.e., Lyft), Chris directly states his sexual boundaries, and Abby
discloses that she has herpes, clearly terrified about how Chris will respond.
Chris handles it with grace and shirks any shameful language. In a touching
moment when they exit the vehicle, the driver also discloses that they have
herpes as well. Afterward, Abby and her friend Campbell are discussing Abby
and Chris's sexual encounter, and there is a jump cut to a visibly queer person
reading *A Recursive Nature*[2] in the same diner, clearly eavesdropping and
smiling about the conversation. In this same episode, Abby attends brunch
with Chris' friends, whose relationship dynamics appear as a smorgasbord of
polyamory and queer relationship structures in addition to queer aesthetics,
with many attendees dressed as elves or fairies. Polyamory is thoughtfully
approached in both *Gen Q* and *Work in Progress*. The original *L Word* suggested that lesbians were too sexual to remain monogamous, but the series
did not necessarily posit nonmonogamy as a valid relationship structure,

constructing nonmonogamous characters such as Shane and Bette as dabbling in infidelity and causing harm to their partners. While *Gen Q* certainly uses heteronormative relationship goals to center main storylines—such as the engagement of Dani and Sophie—the show also portrays nonmonogamous relationships, such as the "throuple" among Alice, Nat, and Gigi.

Gen Q makes numerous improvements in the representations of racialized and/or disabled people whereas *Work in Progress* addresses race and disability through supporting plots and characters, but not in the main narratives. Streitmatter (2009) argues that *The L Word* communicates that the lesbian community is racially diverse, and indeed this continues in *Gen Q*. Furthermore, Bette and her daughter Angie have a frank, emotional conversation about racial disparities and discrimination when Angie is unfairly suspended by her private school for fighting with a bully. *Work in Progress* represents racial diversity in the gathering scene(s) with Chris's friends. Moreover, Abby's ex-partner Melanie is a black woman, and Abby's stepmother and stepsiblings are African American. Abby's overbearing coworker (Susan, played by Mary Sohn) is Asian. However, *Work in Progress* still prioritizes and centers on white characters.

Similar progress was made on *Gen Q* in the casting and representation of people with disabilities. One of the only representations of disability on *The L Word* comes in Season Three, when Marlee Matlin, a deaf woman, is cast as Bette's love interest. In *Gen Q*, Jillian Mercado, who has muscular dystrophy and uses a wheelchair, was cast as Maribel, Sophie's sister and confidante. However, *Gen Q* does not directly acknowledge or discuss disability, and as many media studies scholars have stated, meaningful representation involves more than simply casting members of marginalized groups (Waggoner, 2018). Rather, the ways the media portrays marginalized people—particularly how their roles are integrated into storylines—should become the focal point.

Abby's identity and frankness about having mental illness is certainly important; however, physical disabilities are not as visible on the show. During one scene in Episode Four, Abby has a breakdown in a public bathroom and insults a person in a wheelchair, who quickly retorts "disabled people are not the yardstick to measure how much shittier your life could be" (23:37-23:42). When discussing issues around accessibility, the conversation tends to focus on the difficulties gender-nonconforming and trans people face when accessing public spaces such as bathrooms. The series misses an opportunity to portray a more direct conversation about disabilities of all kinds; however, this focus does complicate notions of accessibility and how certain identities can be disabling, allowing for disidentification between marginalized social groups, such as people with disabilities and gender-nonconforming people. Schalk (2013) defines disidentification "as a third identification stance in relation to dominant ideology that refuses to either fully conform or fully resist," and that is a "strategic survival strategy of identification for/of/ by those with multiple intersecting marginal identities" (p. 4). Disidentifying allows for an acknowledgment of similarities and a commitment to draw connections with, and ultimately commit to resist, oppressive or discriminatory behaviors faced by both communities.

In the digital age, social media and fan engagement play a huge role in the success of a program, with growing examples of participatory culture (Jenkins et. al, 2015) in which fans have responded to content in ways that ultimately embed them in the production of a program (Macklem, 2014; Stein, 2015; Waggoner, 2018). As Waggoner (2018) argues,

> whereas LGBTQ persons previously did not get much of a voice on their media representation, social media platforms allow for better and more globally effective communication practices in attempting to challenge producers and creators and to warrant a need for change. (p. 1877–1878)

Fans of *The L Word* and the dedication of its fan base to its reboot a decade later are certainly an excellent example of this. As such, there is a need for more research on the convergence of television with social media platforms and how online fan communities may influence media production practices (Slade et al., 2015).

The dialogue, storylines, and character development on *Work in Progress* arguably appear more attuned to the goings-on of contemporary queer communities, particularly younger people, and those participating in online queer culture. In comparison, *Gen Q* boasts a similarly "retro feel" compared to its predecessor, as Gordon-Loebl (2020) writes:

> I suspect that the more influential factor in the show's retro feel is that the original *L Word* was a series that was only willing to include the dimensions of queer culture that were already safe to show on mainstream television. That concession to marketability meant that, just like a new car that loses half of its value the minute it's driven off the lot, the show was practically dated by the time it aired. Because queer activists, advocates, and artists are constantly fighting to expand the bounds of queer visibility, if television shows like *The L Word* only ever depict the battles that have already been won, they'll always be behind. (n.p.)

Streitmatter (2009) quotes popular queer website *AfterEllen.com*, as stating that "from a marketing perspective, there is no way 'The L Word' could be accurate and be a success. . . . This show is subject to the same conventions as all of television" (p. 157). As previously discussed, show creator Ilene Chaiken shirked any social responsibility with *The L Word*; to make socially responsible television seemed to be "too much" for broadcast media, primarily a for-profit industry (Waggoner, 2018). In contrast, in a nod to the final scene of *Work in Progress'* last episode of Season One, Gregory (2020) expresses that *Work in Progress* embraces what often makes the queer community "too much," highlighting such intensity as a key component of the show.

Abby McEnany states in an interview with *Indiewire* that a critical element of *Work in Progress* is that "it's not all palatable queers" (Dry, 2020, n.p.). In Episode Eight, Julia Sweeney—Abby's nemesis-turned-acquaintance—reinvents her character "Pat" for a live storytelling event. While well-intentioned, Abby insists that Sweeney's positionality as a cis-gendered heterosexual woman playing a genderqueer nerd means that her characterization gives a "free pass" for the audience to laugh at people like Pat, and by extension, Abby. This tense interaction between Abby and Julia highlights the main argument of this chapter: it is harmful to approach representations of marginalized communities without care, and it is reckless not to consider input from the communities being represented on screen. Increased visibility does not immediately equate to more diverse representations (Waggoner, 2018), and the few representations offered to marginalized communities have a responsibility to these social groups due to the potential influence of such visibility. Both *The L Word: Generation Q* and *Work in Progress* were renewed for a second season; therefore, it is not that shows using unpalatable queers to highlight what makes queer communities "too much" are not sustainable or profitable. If anything, viewers want more.

NOTES

1. A deadname is the name given to an individual at birth which the individual no longer identifies with. For more, see Clements (2017).

2. *A Recursive Nature* (written by Denise Conca) is an explicit fictional novel about the sexual escapades of a middle-aged leather dyke in San Francisco.

REFERENCES

Akass, K. & McCabe, J. (Eds.). (2006). *Reading the L word: Outing contemporary television*. I.B. Tauris.

Berman, J. (2019, December 5). *The L word: Generation Q is a valiant effort. But the show is a time capsule that should have stayed buried*. Time. https://www.time.com/5744710/the-l-word-generation-q-review

Brown, H. & Herndon, A. M. (2020). No bad fatties allowed? Negotiating the meaning and power of the mutable body. In M. Friedman, C. Rice & J. Rinaldi (Eds.), *Thickening fat: Fat bodies, intersectionality, and social justice* (pp. 139–149). Routledge.

Burns, K. & Davies, C. (2009). Producing cosmopolitan sexual citizens on *The L Word*. *Journal of Lesbian Studies, 13*(2), 174–188.

Cefai, S. (2014). Feeling and the production of lesbian space in *The L Word*. *Gender, Place & Culture, 21*(5), 650–665.

Chawansky, M. & Francombe, J. (2013). Wanting to be Anna: Examining lesbian sporting celebrity on *The L Word*. *Journal of Lesbian Studies 17*(2), 134–149.

Clements, K. C. (2017, October 19). *What is deadnaming?* Healthline. https://www.healthline.com/health/transgender/deadnaming

Cooper, C. (2016). *Fat activism: A radical social movement*. HammerOn Press.

Cwynar-Horta, J. (2016). The commodification of the body positive movement on Instagram. *Stream: Culture/Politics/Technology, 8*(2), 36–56.

Dry, J. (2020, January 26) *'Work in progress': How Abby McEnany made the most radical queer show on TV*. IndieWire. https://www.indiewire.com/2020/01/work-in-progress-abby-mcenany-interview-showtime-lesbian-lgbt-1202206057

Gerbner, G. & L. Gross. (1976). Living with television: The violence profile. *Journal of Communication, 26*(2), 173–199.

Giovanelli, D. & Ostertag, S. (2009). Controlling the body: Media representations, body size and self-discipline. In E. Rothblum & S. Solovay (Eds.), *The fat studies reader* (pp. 289–298). NYU Press.

Glock, A. (2005, February 6). *She likes to watch*. The New York Times. https://www.nytimes.com/2005/02/06/arts/television/she-likes-to-watch.html

Gordon-Loebl, N. (2020, February 12). *'The L word: Generation Q' Is a queer soap opera and there's nothing wrong with that*. The Nation. https://www.thenation.com/article/culture/l-word-generation-q-tv-review

Gregory, D. (2020, January 30). *"Work in progress" is too much and so am I*. AutoStraddle. https://www.autostraddle.com/work-in-progress-is-too-much-and-so-am-i

Gross, L. (1991). Out of the mainstream: Sexual minorities and the mass media. *Journal of Homosexuality, 21*(1–2): 19–46.

Guthrie, J. A., Kunkel, A. & Hladky, K. N. (2013). The complex relationship between (and within) the oppressed and the empowered: Contradiction and LGBT portrayals on *The L Word*. In J. Campbell & T. Carilli (Eds.), *Queer media images: LGBT perspectives* (pp. 19–30). Lexington Books.

Heller, D. (2014). Wrecked: Programmed celesbian reality. In B. R. Weber (Ed.). *Reality gendervision: Sexuality and gender on transatlantic reality television* (pp. 123–146). Duke University Press.

Hyndman, J. (2019, August 24). *The L word: Generation Q trailer is here, and it's… queer*. AfterEllen.com. https://www.afterellen.com/tv/571655-the-l-word-generation-q-trailer-is-here-and-its-queer

Jenkins, H., Ito, M. & boyd, d. (2015). *Participatory culture in a networked era: A conversation on youth, learning, commerce, and politics* (1st ed.). Polity Press.

Kern, R. (2012). Andro-phobia? When gender queer is too queer for *L Word* audiences. In K. Ross (Ed.). *The handbook of gender, sex, and media* (pp. 241–259). John Wiley & Sons Ltd.

Macklem, L. (2014). I see what you did there: *SPN* and the fourth wall. In L. Zubernis & K. Larsen (Eds.), *Fan phenomena: Supernatural* (pp. 34–45). Intellect Ltd.

McFadden, M. (2010). 'L' is for looking again: Art and representation on *The L Word. Feminist Media Studies, 10*(4), 421–439.

Moore, C. (2007). Having it all ways: The tourist, the traveler, and the local in *The L Word. Cinema Journal, 46*(4), 3–23.

Padva, G. (2014). *Queer nostalgia in cinema and pop culture.* Palgrave Macmillan.

Schalk, S. (2013). Coming to claim crip: Disidentification with/in disability studies. *Disability Studies Quarterly, 33*(2), 22.

Sedgwick, E. K. (2004). *The L Word*: Novelty and normalcy. *Chronicle of Higher Education 50*(19), B10–B11.

Slade, A. F., Narro, A. J. & Givens-Carroll, D. (Eds.). (2015). *Television, social media, and fan culture.* Lexington Books.

Stein, L. E. (2015). *Millennium fandom.* University of Iowa Press.

Streitmatter, R. (2009). *From 'perverts' to 'fab five': The media's changing depiction of gay men and lesbians.* Routledge.

Topel, F. (2019, September 20). *How the L word: Generation Q will address modern day LGBTQ issues.* Cheatsheet. https://www.cheatsheet.com/entertainment/how-the-l-word-generation-q-will-address-modern-day-lgbtq-issues.html

Tuchman, G., Daniels, A. & J. Benet (Eds.). (1978). *Hearth and home: Images of women in the mass media.* Oxford Press.

USC Annenberg School for Communication and Journalism. (n.d.). *Key concepts.* The Critical Media Project. https://www.criticalmediaproject.org/about/key-concepts

Waggoner, E. B. (2018). Bury your gays and social media fan response: Television, LGBTQ representation, and communitarian ethics. *Journal of Homosexuality, 65*(13), 1877–1891.

Walker, A. (2019). *The L Word: Generation Q's Marja-Lewis Ryan on Diversity and Avoiding Tokenism.* Advocate. https://www.advocate.com/television/2019/7/25/l-word-reboots-marja-lewis-ryan-diversity-avoiding-tokenism

Webster, M. (2019, August 28). *My hopes and fears for the L word: Generation Q.* AfterEllen.com. https://www.afterellen.com/general-news/572017-my-hopes-and-fears-for-the-l-word-generation-q

Chapter 4

Race, Poverty, and Narco-capitalism on *The Wire*

A Political-Economic Analysis

Michael Johnson, Jr.

This chapter will critically examine how poverty and race function in tandem within the narrative world of HBO's award-winning series *The Wire* (Simon et al., 1999–2007). I will analyze the series across its five seasons, with a special focus on the series' interpretation of poverty, race, and narco-capitalism within the upwardly mobile economic aspirations of many of its characters, its impoverished geographic setting, and the drug distribution and consumption landscape of Baltimore. *The Wire*'s setting also offers viewers an interpretation of a contemporary urban metropolis populated with African American and Latinx citizens who occupy the bottom of the socioeconomic spectrum, while city politicians, judicial officers, and businessmen occupy the highest echelons of that hierarchy. Using textual and discourse analysis, I critically analyze the messages the series offers to its audience in keeping with an intersectional (Crenshaw, 1991) theoretical framework. To accomplish this intersectional analysis, I explicitly eschew attempts to eradicate identity categories we colloquially refer to as "race" and socioeconomic "class" and instead use them to draw linkages between these two concepts in tandem with a theory of poverty because understanding the complexities between these connections "can instead be the source of social empowerment and reconstruction" (Crenshaw, 1991, p. 1242). This is especially true when one considers the factual parallels between racial underrepresentation and impoverished socioeconomic standing within the United States. Thus, adopting this framework can illuminate how messages in mass media can shed light on convenient one-dimensional construction of the human experience that is "often shaped by other dimensions of their identities" outside of the conventional Hollywood formula.

This chapter's analysis will attempt to answer the following three questions. First, how is the socioeconomic hierarchy defined within the series and in what discrete ways is poverty defined? How are those definitions contested or reaffirmed against its inner-city setting, and by whom? Second, what influence, if any, does the narco-capitalist system of drug production, distribution, and consumption have upon the characters' lives? And third, how are wealth and success characterized and by whom? What justifications (if any) are offered for the methods by which their economic successes are achieved, and what costs (if any) are attached to those successes?

The use of textual analysis focused on discursive forces present in a text is an important means of understanding how individuals and society constitute themselves and make sense of the larger world in which they live. Textual analysis can usefully interrogate how mass-mediated commodities create identities and "construct authoritative truths" (Saukko, 2003) for those who use them, thereby illuminating the participatory (or nonparticipatory) role social actors possess in the creation, reflection, and consumption of those truths. The multiple interpretations of a given "text" frequently look different when examined in relation to other texts or social sensibilities; thus, the task of analysis is not to ascertain *the most correct*, but rather, to explore some of the possible and undiscovered interpretations embedded in the targets of textual analysis. This chapter's intersectional framework is employed to examine how exchanges of both financial and social capital, along with socioeconomic labor practices, give rise to (or undermine) different forms of social relations between racial minorities and whites, as well as between the wealthy and impoverished on the series. Additionally, I utilize some basic premises of critical race theory to augment this political-economic analysis. This chapter adopts as axiomatic that institutional racism is "original and not aberrational" and is the "usual way society does business, the common everyday experience of most people of color in this country" (Delgado & Stefancic, 2012, p. 7). Moreover, I also integrate the belief that our socioeconomic systems adopt a "white-over-color" partiality that "serves important purposes, both psychic and material, for the dominant group" because such institutional racism manifests itself by advancing the interests of "both white elites (materially) and working class Caucasians (psychically)." Thus, the majority of American society has little incentive to eradicate such a structure (Delgado & Stefancic, 2012, p. 8). Finally, I utilize the concept of "color blind racism," whereby conceptions of equality are "expressed in rules that insist only on treatment that is the same across the board, and can thus remedy *only the most blatant forms* of discrimination" [my emphasis] (Delgado & Stefancic, 2012, p. 8; Bonilla-Silva, 2013). Together, these tools offer a robust analysis that interprets the series' characters and their actions within a much larger, multiple-season narrative, unlike every other crime drama previously found on American television to date.

The Wire is a political polemic that critiques several institutions located throughout the city of Baltimore, where the story begins. *The Wire* is a contemporary crime drama centered upon the lives of the city's citizens. But over five seasons and 60 episodes, it ultimately evolves from its pure crime drama origins, dedicated to investigating and commenting upon the illegal drug trade in Baltimore, to later include complex analyses of the Baltimore economy through its Harbor, Ports, and longshoremen (Season Two), its internally inept city government and the cronyism of the political system upon which it relies (Season Three), the city's woefully dysfunctional educational systems (Season Four), and finally the capitalist fallibility of the city's major newspaper (Season Five). Throughout the series, however, an important thread links these various seasons with the organized drug syndicate that has infiltrated all these institutions. For the purposes of this analysis, however, it is imperative that we recognize that the series "replicates a common genre convention that situates all criminality in poor urban communities stereotypically populated by racial minorities who are either unemployed or underemployed or trapped in normative middle-class jobs of respectability" (Johnson Jr., 2013).

From the very first episode of the series, audiences are confronted with a stark and unavoidable fact, and that is that Baltimore is a city defined by three things: drugs, minorities, and economic inequality, though not necessarily in that order. From the very first scene of "The Target," the first episode of the series (Simon et al., 2002), we find a crime scene in a bloody inner-city street and a discussion about the murder of an anonymous black man by the name of Omar Bets, shot upon a landscape in the background of abandoned and boarded-up brick row houses (1:16). Only a few moments later, viewers are transported to the marble-lined hallways of a courthouse and the wood-paneled walls with frosted glass chandeliers of a Baltimore City Circuit courtroom, resplendent with the suits and ties of attorneys, and the muted-color attire of solidly respectable middle-class jurors (5:50). Even in these very first, but formative, few minutes of the very first episode, the racial politics are as equally visible as its socioeconomic moments. Both on the streets and in the courthouse we see the Irish American Detective Jimmy McNulty, along with any number of a cast of white characters who occupy the middle- and upper-class echelons of the series' society, to include: Jewish defense attorney Maurice Levy (04:49), white judge Daniel Phelan (05:06), white assistant district attorney Rhonda Pearlman (05:33), white state's attorney Steven Demper (08:57), white homicide sergeant Jay Landsman (21:02), and white careerist Major William A. "Bill" Rawls (22:00). With a few exceptions, they all conveniently contrast with the homogenous African American criminal characters of the series in the form of D'Angelo Barksdale, Stringer Bell, Omar Little, and their gang associates (12:50–13:10), who repeatedly make their appearances throughout the episode in not nearly as prestigious settings, such as strip clubs (26:30), street corners, and housing projects (34:50). Thus, the series establishes its socioeconomic settings early on by drawing very visible distinctions that closely parallel racial lines with the generally white hierarchies of socially respectable careers like law enforcement and the judicial and legal professions, against those of the nearly hegemonic African American narco-capitalist criminal enterprises of inner-city Baltimore. According to Martha Nochimson, McNaulty's story is only peripheral to the narrative of Season One's story, and McNaulty is only

> one element of a big collage composed of juxtaposed stories and points of view. McNaulty's striving to be a hero is part of a live mosaic of perspectives emanating from the essentially white middle/upper-class community and from the essentially black poor/lower-class community. (2019, pp. 95–96)

David Simon, the primary showrunner and producer of the series, made decisions that

> reflect a conscious desire to choose individuals to play specific characters based upon the conformity of the actors phenotypical appearance and congruence with the idea of who those characters were and how they should appear, behave, and exist within *The Wire*'s story world. (Johnson Jr., 2013)

In fact, realism is so persuasive that Brian Rose comments that Simon, in a type of self-congratulatory way, "fondly notes a strong following among both cops and criminals who admire the show's faithful recreation of their lives" (Rose, 2008). These characters reflect a conscious decision about how the series wishes its story to be told that is in keeping with a *very specific agenda* to convince audiences of its realism. That realism relies upon a number of racial (Dixon, 2008; McDermott, 2006) and socioeconomic (Kendall, 2011; Murphy, 2014) stereotypes that are repeated from the very beginning. And, as Rabia Belt poignantly observes, while the series is "rightly praised for its faithful and respectful treatment of urban poverty, we should however remind ourselves that *The Wire* is a created domain and does not show a comprehensive picture of life as a citizen of Baltimore" (2012, p. 3). Moreover, the series' strength lies in its ability to "question, among other things, the comforting formulaic expectations that TV has associated with both heroes and science" (Nochimson, 2019, p. 94). And as I previously noted, the series "is as much about the narco-capitalist drug economy as it is about that economy's participants. The class-based politics embedded in the series' plots and dialogue expose an important area for discussion insofar as urban criminality is related to race" (2013).

Without the Barksdale narco-criminal enterprise central to the series, many other adjacent businesses (like the strip clubs and entertainment sectors) and government agencies (like law enforcement, judicial, and harbor transportation industry) would find themselves struggling to exist (or at least remain socially relevant). *The Wire* points to Baltimore's real-world transition from an economy "based on physical labor and tangible products to one based more on information, technology, and services as the displacing agent that turns drug dealing into a logical occupational decision" (Long, 2008). The socioeconomic class structure, established very early in the series' first season, is reinforced in later episodes (and not *just* in terms of its characters of color), but also for the series' working-class immigrants and wealthy Caucasian and Jewish characters as well. Audiences are introduced to the ubiquity of institutional dysfunction that permeates *The Wire* narrative, and that relies upon equally potent socioeconomic inequalities. Nochimson notes:

> The early episodes introduce us . . . [to] a city too poor to conduct police and court business properly; a drug trade well organized by Barksdale and Bell; large numbers of hopeless people in the drug scene caught up in addiction; police, underpaid, demoralized, and lacking [financial] resources; and careerists, daunted by an impossible and racist economy, fighting for a foothold on the professional ladder, whether or not their efforts run counter to the job they were hired to do. (2019, p. 96)

What is significant about Season One is the ubiquity of the poor within the inner-city confines of the series. They exist and are seen against the landscape and form the background against which the narrative's action takes place. Whether seen in the high-rise apartment projects or the low-rise ghettos, alleyways, and streets, the impoverished are everywhere. However, few truly *homeless* characters ever appear for any significant length of time in speaking roles and none (with one notable exception) over the course of the series' five seasons. Thus, the poor are everywhere, but remain for the most part a voiceless component of the background.

Therefore, for the purposes of this analysis, I examine just how the poor are constituted, through a close examination of one Reginald "Bubbles" Cousins, a middle-aged African American man and

> lifelong drug user who has miraculously maintained an active sense of responsibility despite his dependence on drugs . . . [he] is a police informer, and the police he works for promise him protection . . . but [financial] pressures

on the police keep them from coming to his aid when he needs them most. (Nochimson, 2019, pp. 106–107)

Bubbles is not *technically* homeless, as many drug addicts of the series are housed in a state of semi-permanency within the innumerable abandoned rowhomes that populate the landscape of the inner city where most of the episodes occur. Despite this fact, the homeless, due to their drug addictions, inadvertently become an indispensable part of the narco-capitalist system of commerce. These overwhelmingly African American homeless drug addicts are uniformly "invisible, except when presented as faceless statistics or as 'problems' to be dealt with in a community" (Kendall, 2011, p. 82), but their framing by Simon et al., follow a predictable pattern by which the poor are depicted "in terms of personal experience; where the viewer is provided with a particular [episode] of an individual or family living under economic duress" (Gilbert, 2011).

Bubbles' story follows this pattern but is an important component of the narrative, although Simon's attentiveness to this demographic follows a framing of the issue of that "gives poverty a human face but often ignores the larger structural factors" (Kendall, 2011, p. 83). In Season One we find Bubbles having been recently released from prison three months prior to the start of the series. He is currently using counterfeit money in a desperate attempt to buy heroin from Barksdale dealers in the local housing project. D'Angelo Barksdale (the leader of the Barksdale drug organization) recognizes the fake currency and instructs his dealers to punish its use. Johnny Weeks, another heroin addict and protégé of Bubbles, attempts to use the fake cash but is ultimately caught by the dealers and severely punished. The discovery by Bubbles of Johnny's abuse moves him to inform on the Barksdale criminal organization through his contact with Detective Shakima Greggs. His service as a confidential informant proves highly valuable to the police department by identifying dealers, explaining events that transpire, and recalling details such as dates and locations important to the successful operation of the Barksdale organization. This service is rewarded with an ongoing financial reward that proves invaluable to his survival. Although drug addiction is a major subtext of the entire series, drug addiction *itself* is not investigated with any seriousness; however, the *socioeconomic effects* that such drug consumption produces *are central* to the narrative. *The Wire*'s success comes from its ability to offer up characters with whom we might identify or to whom we are attracted and invested in seeing more of, and Bubbles' unassuming appearance and secretly powerful knowledge make us want to cheer for his survival throughout the series.

Bubbles suffers through several minor interactions with police through Seasons One and Two, such that by Season Three we find him actively selling t-shirts to young dealers on the streets. His sales as a street vendor continue through Season Four (now pushing a cart named "Bubbles' Depot"), as does his service as a confidential informant, thereby augmenting his survival. Debating his ability to survive the brutal conditions of the street, he says to his business partner and fellow addict Sherrod:

> 21:16 – 22:11: If I can cut you loose to handle the money, I can cover twice the ground, selling twice the merchandise . . . more of what you would call, uhh, market share. Instead, I have to keep your ass close. You should have been moved on to your own (shopping) cart by now! You have to step up the math skills if you want to advance in this here enterprise. (Burns et al. 2006b)

Bubbles may be a heroin addict, but he is well aware of the mechanics of the capitalist economy in which he is inextricably linked. However, characters like Bubbles—because he serves as the most visible proxy for the truly poor—run the risk of mischaracterizing poverty as an individualized problem and drug addiction as a personal failure rather than a systemic problem. In the fourth episode of Season Four (Burns et al. 2006a), Bubble reminisces about his childhood, saying that "everything changes . . . one moment the ice cream truck is the only thing you want to hear," and in the next he is an addict pushing a shopping cart (52:39). Later, as Bubbles surveys his meager earnings selling his shopping cart commodities, we see that he and his partner are living in a cinder-block garage where he sleeps with his shopping cart and an electric extension cord providing light while cooking over a charcoal grill.

After the death of his friend Sherrod, the police department officials take pity on Bubbles, and rather than involve him in the death, Bubbles is instead committed to a state psychiatric facility in lieu of his facing jail time for Sherrod's overdose. But by *The Wire*'s fifth and final season, Bubbles has been clean for over a year and is living in his sister Rae's basement, earning money selling newspapers on the street.

Here poverty, race, and the criminality of drug addiction coalesce in Bubbles' life history that speaks to the power of narco-capitalism at the intersections of race and poverty. Poverty is thus inextricably linked to the African American characters, who overwhelmingly occupy Baltimore's lowest and most vulnerable population—the drug-addicted homeless of the city. Although Bubbles escapes his drug addiction, at the expense of his freedom, he nevertheless finds himself stuck, literally, at the bottom by living in his sister's basement without the ability to enter her home except during the hours when she is home from work. Thus, his character in many ways represents how middle-class society's distrust of the criminal addict transgresses racial lines, but not socioeconomic ones. His sister's fears are exemplified in the following exchange between the two from the first episode of Season Five

(Simon et al., 2008), where Bubbles asks to stay home as his sister is about to leave for work:

32:30: I'm going to work; you know I've got night shift all this week.

32:37: You know I can stay down here quiet like, we don't need to fight.

32:41: You don't stay here when I'm not around, that's our rule.

32:45: I'm your brother Rae, I've got nowhere to go when I leave here.

32:49: The last time I left you alone in my home, you dragged half my kitchen to a pawnshop. You remember that!?

(Pause)

32:58: But you can keep the door locked right? I'm down here.

33:01: *My rules*—you said.

(Bubbles packs up his things and walks out the basement back door. After hearing his departure, Rae turns off the basement light and closes the door at the top of the stairs.)

Bubbles' story eventually finds its way to publicity in the form of a *Baltimore Sun* newspaper reporter, who publishes an account of Bubbles' life. And eventually, after reading about her brother's story in the newspaper, Rae invites him up the stairs (and back into her life). When only *one* character, like Bubbles, survives the five seasons of the series, audiences run the risk of interpreting such characters as sympathetic exceptions, thereby creating the impression that anyone in a similar situation can escape poverty (Kendall, 2011, p. 111). Moreover, it speaks volumes that it takes *five seasons* for Bubbles to permanently escape the poverty that he has experienced for the duration of the series, feeding stereotypes of highly racialized homelessness and drug addiction in one neat character. But contradictorily, a number of unique factors weigh in Bubbles' favor and obscure the costs associated with his reintroduction to society, costs which in reality are very high. The fictional depiction of homelessness, addiction, and race represented by his character belies the facts in contemporary America. For instance, Ben Johnson (2019) notes a study conducted by the U.S. Department of Housing and Urban Development that shows that while approximately 500,000 Americans were homeless at any given point, only 35% were living on the street, while 65% were living in temporary housing like shelters. And unlike Baltimore, almost half (47%) of the homeless population reside in the state of California, though many cities on the East Coast have the highest *rates* of homelessness. Sixteen percent of this demographic of American society suffers from chronic substance abuse, but even for Americans without this problem, Family Promise notes that almost "60% of Americans will spend at least one year below the poverty line at some point between the ages of 25 and 75." Although Bubbles represents to *The Wire's* viewers what poverty is supposed to look like, the fact is that "more than 15% of Americans live in poverty," and it is families, not individuals, who comprise almost 40% of the entire homeless population. However, Bubbles does factually represent the racial composition of the homeless and impoverished population because 40% of that demographic (and 49% of homeless families) is composed of African Americans, despite occupying only 12.5% of the American population (Jones, 2016, p. 140). What is significant about this fact is that the racial overrepresentation in the homeless population has remained unchanged since 1985. But when it comes to the racial demographics of heroin addiction—which comprised 37.5% of drug overdose deaths (second only to prescription opioids), the picture is far less clear.

The Wire's depiction of Bubbles' addiction goes almost completely uncontested in terms of race. Almost all the heroin addicts of the series are seen to be phenotypically homogenous African Americans, with Johnny Weeks from the first three seasons being the only exception over the course of the series' five seasons. Moreover, it is Walon (played by the white, actual former heroin addict Steve Earle) who helps fulfill the white savior trope by serving as Bubbles' Narcotics Anonymous sponsor to help him escape his addiction. But Bruce D. Johnson argues that "many unstated connotations are symbolically linked to the concepts of 'heroin' and 'addiction'" that are frequently "ignored or forgotten by the public, equating 'black' and 'criminal' with 'addict'" (Johnson, 1977, p. 52). Most significantly for this analysis is that Johnson argues about the confluence of race and addiction with *The Wire*'s depiction of these concepts in the popular consciousness:

> Three myths are briefly analyzed here . . . blacks are more likely than whites to be addicts; lower-class persons are more likely than middle class persons to be addicts; and those who have ever been addicted are very likely to remain addicted . . . [however] Blacks are only likely to be addicts if (a) the comparison of whites is skipped, (b) the small proportions of both Blacks and Whites are ignored, and (c) the current use of heroin is equated with *addiction* [emphasis added]. (1997, p. 52).

His research also dispels some of the other assumptions about socioeconomic classes that have been replicated some 40 years later, namely when observing that

> unemployed Whites are almost as likely to try heroin as their Black counterparts. For Whites, the lower the social class the more the heroin use; among Blacks, however, heroin is less strongly linked to class. Moreover, these measures of class (highest education and present employment) are not very helpful in predicting how to prevent heroin use, since they frequently occur long after heroin use has begun. (1977, p. 53)

Notably then, it is sad reassurance to find that seven years after *The Wire*'s conclusion, Martins et al. found that "recent data indicates . . . Whites are overrepresented among heroin/opioid-related fatal overdose cases" (2015, pp. 278–279). Certainly, the Barksdale/Stanfield criminal organizations have benefited from the drug trade on the series, but the users of their products do not appear to mirror those typically found on the streets of Baltimore today, despite the laudatory rhetoric the series has produced in the form of industry awards and popular acclaim.

The much more common depiction of poverty on *The Wire* takes the form of the *working-class poor*, whose existence is often framed in the media as "low-skill manual workers, people employed in routine white-collar jobs (such as bank clerks, cashiers, and retail sales), and in the rapidly- growing service sector (for instance home health care workers, and employees in fast-food restaurants)" (Kendall, 2011, p. 123). These *working-class poor* appear on the series but often do not follow Kendall's definition because they are uniformly employed in occupations that typically require advanced skills, knowledge, and abilities, or college degrees (as is the case in Seasons Four and Five in which secondary school teachers and journalists appear). Their impoverishment is not defined by occupation but rather by the atypically low compensation that accompanies their underfunded or economically unprofit-able institutions—in this case the Baltimore City Police Department. To all appearances the *working-class poor* of the series includes low level police officers, high school teachers, and print journalists—all of whom normally would occupy a solidly *middle-class status* according to most definitions like those articulated by Kendall:

> Even under the best of circumstances, the working poor hold low-wage posi-tions with little job security, few employee benefits, and no chance to save money. Their work conditions are frequently unpleasant and sometimes danger-ous, and significantly, they are also "only a step—or a second family income—away from poverty. (2011, p. 124)

However, this precarity is notably absent for those members of the legal profession and the higher-level police administration like the white Major William Rawls or, white FBI special agent Terrence "Fitz" Fitzhugh who first appear on Season One, and who possess either a college education or advanced degrees in the law. From the (white) Councilmen Thomas Carcetti to the (white) State Attorney Steven Demper to the (white) ADA Rhonda Pearlman the majority of the Caucasian characters occupy the upper echelons of the socioeconomic strata and thus are relatively free of the insecurity and precarity experienced by the racially mixed "underclass" (Katz, 2013) found in the Baltimore City Police Department.

These solidly middle-class characters reflect many of the characteristics and traits one expects: they appear to earn between $40k and $62k based on appearances and possessions like homeownership and clothing (Kendall, 2011, p. 165). Many of these characters reflect the kinds of cosmopolitan values, egalitarian expectations, and upwardly mobile aspirations of that socio-economic stratum of society as indicated by their behavior (and reaction) to many of the systemic institutional and cultural problems they regularly face. And in keeping with prevailing class distinctions in America, they generally consist of characters who "have some college education or significant skills and work under loose supervision, and the upper-middle-class consisting of highly educated professionals and corporate managers" (Gilbert, 2011) with some in the upper-middle-class or wealthy demographic whose social life reproduces the kinds of adaptability in shifting cultural norms of propriety, by demonstrable evidence of social cultivation, workplace social interactions, dress, appearance, grooming, and the accoutrements of social sophistication. Throughout *The Wire*, they reproduce the traits and values that are associated with the middle class such as "punctuality, a certain minimum of reliability and accountability (if not responsibility), as well as a minimum of orderliness and a certain amount of postponement of instant gratification" (Ehrenreich, 1990) as well as the values of individualism, achievement and success, progress and material comfort, and freedom of liberty (Williams Jr., 1970). These depictions are rendered visible in the cases of many characters: (African American) Lt. Cedric Daniels and his girlfriend the (white) Assistant District Attorney Rhonda Pearlman, (African American) Major Howard "Bunny" Colvin, (white) Major William Rawls, and many others. All of them share in the expectations of economic security and safety, protections strongly associated with this demographic and poignantly illustrated by a recent report entitled *Middle-Class Task Force* (Blank, 2010) that persuasively argues that these values include:

1. Strong orientation toward planning for the future.
2. Control over one's destiny.
3. Movement up the socioeconomic ladder through hard work and education.
4. A well-rounded education for one's children.
5. Protection against hardship, including crime, poverty, and health problems.
6. Access to homeownership and financial assets such as a savings account.

In every case, we find that the preceding characters are all uniformly preoccupied with future advancement, and they actively pursue a future with discrete goals in mind. They are equipped with the ability, due to their positions in their respective careers, to exercise some degree of control over their future, and by the end of the series, they have all moved up within their respective occupations. By *The Wire*'s final season, many of the narrative threads have been concluded, and the HBO audience is left with the feeling that life has improved for most of the series' characters. But what other messages has *The Wire* conveyed to America about what poverty looks like, what the poor must do to survive, and how people are responding to the inherent instability of their socioeconomic positions? There is no question that we are left with a complicated and at times false impression about these issues, despite the gripping drama that the series creates with its fictional accounts of life at the bottom of our social hierarchy.

REFERENCES

Belt, R. (2012). 'And then comes life': The intersection of race, poverty, and disability in HBO's *The Wire*. *Rutgers Race and Law Review, 13*(2), 409–435.

Blank, R. M. (2010). *Middle Class in America*. U.S. Department of Commerce. https://www.commerce.gov/data-and-reports/reports/2010/01/middle-class-amer ica

Bonilla-Silva, E. (2013). *Racism without racists: Color-Blind racism and the persistence of racial inequality in America*. Rowman & Littlefield.

Burns, E., Lehane, D. (Writers), & McKay, J. (Director). (2006, October 1). Refugees (Season 4, Episode 4) [TV series episode]. In D. Simon, R. F. Colesberry, & N. K. Noble (Executive Producers), The wire. Blown Deadline Productions; HBO.

Burns, E., Mills, D. (Writers), & Moore, C. (Director). (2006, September 17). Soft eyes (Season 4, Episode 2) [TV series episode]. In D. Simon, R.F. Colesberry, & N.K. Noble (Executive Producers), The wire. Blown Deadline Productions; HBO.

Crenshaw, K. (1991, July). Mapping the margins: Intersectionality, Identity politics, and violence against women of color. *Stanford Law Review, 43*(6), 1241–1300.

Delgado, R., & Stefancic, J. (2012). *Critical race theory: An introduction*. New York University Press.

Dixon, T. L. (2008). Network news and racial beliefs: Exploring the connection between national television news exposure and stereotypical perceptions of African Americans. *Journal of Communications, 58*, 321–337.

Ehrenreich, B. (1990). *Fear of falling: The inner life of the middle class*. Harper Perennial.

Family Promise. *Fast facts about homelessness and poverty* (n.d.). https://familyp romise.org/fast-facts-about-homelessness-and-poverty/

Gilbert, D. (2011). *The American class structure in an age of growing inequality* (Eight Edition). Pine Forge Press.

Johnson, B. (2019, September 23). *10 facts about homelessness in America*. Acton Institute. https://www.acton.org/publications/transatlantic/2019/09/23/10-facts-a bout-homelessness-america

Johnson, B. D. (1977). Race, Class, and Irreversibility Hypotheses: Myths and research about heroin. In J. D. Rittenhouse (Ed.), *The epidemiology of heroin and other narcotics* (pp. 51–57). University of Michigan Library.

Johnson Jr., M. (2013). White authorship and the counterfeit politics of verisimilitude on *The Wire*. In D. J. Leonard, & L. A. Guerrero (Eds.), *Race-ing for ratings: African Americans on television* (pp. 324–341). Praeger.

Jones, M. M. (2016). Does race matter in addressing homelessness? A review of the literature. *World Medical Health Policy, 8*(2), 139–156.

Katz, M. B. (2013). *The undeserving poor: American's enduring confrontation with poverty*. Oxford University Press.

Kendall, D. (2011). *Framing class: Media representations of wealth and poverty in America*. Rowman & Littlefield.

Long, A. (2008). *Dealing with drugs: Gender, genre, and seriality in The Wire and Weeds*. University of Florida.

Martins, S. S., Santaella-Tenorio, J., Marshall, B. D., Maldonado, A., & Cerda, M. (2015). Racial/ethnic differences in trends in heroin use and heroin-related risk behaviors among nonmedical prescription opioid users. *Drug and Alcohol Dependence, 151*, 278–283.

McDermott, M. (2006). *Working class white: The making and unmaking of race relations*. University of California Press.

Murphy, N. L. (2014). *Class negotiations: Poverty, welfare policy, and American television*. University of Texas.

Nochimson, M. P. (2019). *Television rewired: The rise of the auteur series*. University of Texas Press.

Rose, B. G. (2008). *The Wire*. In G. R. Edgerton (Ed.), *The essential HBO reader* (pp. 82–91). University Press of Kentucky.

Saukko, P. (2003). *Doing research and cultural studies: An introduction to classical and new methodological approaches*. SAGE.

Simon, D., Burns, E. (Writers), & Chappell, J. (Director). (2008, January 6). More with less (Season 5, Episode 1) [TV series episode]. In D. Simon, R.F. Colesberry, & N.K. Noble (Executive Producers), *The wire*. Blown Deadline Productions; HBO.

Simon, D., Burns, E. (Writers), & Johnson, C. (Director). (2002, June 2). The target (Season 1, Episode 1) [TV series episode]. In D. Simon, R. F. Colesberry, & N. K. Noble (Executive Producers), *The wire*. Blown Deadline Productions; HBO.

Simon, D., Colesberry, R.F., & Kostroff, N.K (Executive Producers). (2002–2008). *The wire* [TV series]. Blown Deadline Productions; HBO.

Williams Jr., R. M. (1970). *American society: A sociological interpretation* (Third Revised Edition). Alfred A. Knopf, Inc.

Chapter 5

The Transgender Super Nanny, *Babysitter Gin*

A Postcolonial Analysis

Kimiko Akita

Delving into Crenshaw's (1994) notion of intersectionality, this chapter explores the intersectional identities of the transgender super nanny Gin, along with her intersectional connections with Japanese women. Though Gin is a fictional character in a *manga* (comic book) and a live actor in a TV drama, she projects an ideal woman's image, a mother whose intersectional identities are obscure in Japanese society. Through Gin's image and performance, interlocking identities of Japanese women (especially mothers) come to light. Crenshaw's notion of intersectionality informs my examination of Gin's identity to uncover the struggles and challenges of sociocultural oppressions that mothers face. A mother/wife is not just a mother/wife, though she may be consigned to the single category of "married woman." She may also have a mother-in-law who is like a "gloved despot" (Plath, 1980, p. 141) or a surveillance camera. She also may be a victim of domestic violence. In Japan, a childless mother, a single mother, or a divorced mother is likely stigmatized. As a mother/wife, she wears a social mask with her family's façade; she is watched and judged by her neighbors, other mothers, and the social gaze because of her attire, makeup, demeanor, speech, and even the *obento* (lunch box) she fixes for her children, since the *obento* represents the mother herself (Allison, 2000, p. 96). The ideal "good wife/wise mother" represses herself to guard her family's privacy and secrets, with any leak having the potential to discredit or tarnish her family's image and reputation. As a result, a mother's domestic life is shielded from outside scrutiny.

Gin is a transgender nanny. She emerged first as a transgender *manga* (comic book) character who was born male, but identified as a bisexual, transgender female. In the television series, Gin is performed by a heterosexual

Japanese male actor who was educated in the UK. Both Gin the *manga* character and Gin the television character act as a dedicated mother to everyone. Gin represents an emergent identity, a "uniquely hybrid creation" (Shields, 2008, p. 305). Her hybrid identity (e.g., a mixture of Western/Eastern culture, man/woman, modern/traditional) allows Gin to assert the voices of mothers, to scold her client's lazy husband, and to openly disagree with her client's mother-in-law in the *manga* and in the TV drama. Although Gin is a woman in everyone's eyes, unlike women, her assertion and transgression are tolerated and considered more credible because of her transgender and biologically male identities, giving her male privilege (see Akita, 2013, p. 94). Gin's emergent identity empowers women characters, women readers, and women audiences. Shields (2008) claims that an intersectional approach could facilitate an understanding of the fluidity in and between and within identity categories (p. 308). Given the strong connection between Gin and Japanese women, Gin's identity comes closer to the image of an ideal Japanese mother, making Japanese women feel closer to her.

Babysitter Gin was a Japanese *shojo* (girls') *manga* published from 1998 to 2007. Gin, a tall, bulky Japanese nanny who dresses like the character Mary Poppins from the eponymous 1964 Walt Disney film, creatively solves family, parenting, and relational problems for her clients. She began the long-running narrative by showing up at her client's door wearing a prim-and-proper woman's black business suit of Victorian-era style, offset by a ruffled white blouse and red bow tie above a long, black, fringed skirt, along with dark sunglasses and a black derby atop her head, carrying an oversized handbag and black umbrella. She proudly and effeminately announces herself as a nanny certified by the British Royal Nanny Association and dispatched by the *Shimo-ochiai* Poppins Agency, which she founded with her inheritance.

Gin is not just any nanny, however. She is a transgender super nanny who performs tasks beyond expectations and without being asked, such as arranging a romantic dinner for parents on the brink of divorce, helping a mother to express breast milk, acting as a midwife, and chasing after a kidnapper's car like a superhero. Contrary to her masculine physique, Gin's demeanor and speech are feminine, sophisticated, and refined. In everyone's eyes, Gin is a woman. Only *manga* readers know that she is transgender. They are immersed in the imaginary, gender-fluid world of Gin and can detach themselves from their own gender and (mostly) heteronormative life.

First published as a *manga* in 1998, *Babysitter Gin* expanded through nine books, for a total of 36 stories by its conclusion in 2007. In 2019, NHK (Japan Broadcasting Corporation) adapted *Babysitter Gin* into a TV series consisting of 10 episodes of 50 minutes each with no intermission, which aired from June 30 to September 1. This TV version, written by Waki Yamato, featuring a singing-and-acting flash mob performed each week by Gin and other characters of all ages, genders, and occupations to appeal to a range of viewers, ultimately ranked fifth among the most-recorded NHK-BS programs in 2019. By comparison, reruns of the U.S.-generated program *Little House on the Prairie* ranked tenth during the same time.

Although both the *manga* and TV versions of *Babysitter Gin* were entertaining, humorous, and emotionally moving, the gender construction of Gin differed between the two media. In the *manga*, Gin's gender identity was outwardly female toward other characters, but fluid to *manga* fans, who understood that Gin was transgender. On the other hand, the TV version clearly accentuates heteronormativity and Gin's biological sex. TV Gin performs as a transgender nanny, but is played by Takuro Ohno, a tall, straight male actor. Despite his willowy and effeminate figure with rosy-red lip gloss and long, supple, black hair, Gin could not fool all TV viewers. Some gender-specific roles appear too dissonant for Ohno to perform. For critical feminist TV spectators (among others), Mr. Ohno's hugging one of Gin's clients or massaging her breast to express milk would have been perceived as sexual assault. Gin also demonstrates her masculinity by punching the air with her fist and treating a woman to a drink in a bar. *Jii*, an elderly and paternalistic butler who appears as Gin's housemate in the TV show only, called Gin "*Bocchama* (young master)" and advised Gin not to cross-dress, signaling to viewers Gin's maleness as heteronormative.

In this chapter, analyzing both the *shojo manga* stories and TV episodes of *Babysitter Gin*, I examine the appeal of Gin's intersectional maternal image and gender identity to consumers via both print and digital media. I apply Taussig's (1993) ideas of *mimetics* and *alterity* in relation to Baudrillard's (1981/1994) notion of *simulacra*, Anderson's (1983) theory of *imagined community*, and Bhabha's (1994) notions of postcolonial and postmodern[1] notions of *hybridity*, *mimesis*, and *ambivalence* to discuss the relationship between *Babysitter Gin* and the drama's consumers in late capitalism.

In male-dominated postwar Japan, *shojo manga* grew popular as an alternative for girls who had been traditionally defined as "not-quite-female," or sexually inexperienced (i.e., virginal) and innocent (Robertson 1998, p. 65). Through reading about boy–girl friendships in *shojo manga*, Japanese girls learned about society's ideal images of them, along with emotional and intimate relationships in general (Prough 2011). *Shojo manga* also provided girls with opportunities to imagine, to dream, and to challenge themselves: enabling them to fantasize about their futures and helping them feel as if they could do anything. Gender-bending characters such as "tomboys" were especially empowering to Japanese girls of that era. In the 1950s and 1960s, *ryosaikenbo*—the traditional stay-at-home "good wife/wise mother" who fully obeyed not only her husband, but also his mother—was the ideal woman. *Shojo manga* enabled girls to immerse themselves in an imaginary world and detach themselves from their real lives. Like Anderson's (1983) *imagined community, shojo manga* readers engaged one another through their shared imagination and fantasy without meeting one another face-to-face.

Shojo manga evolved from its "golden age" of the 1950s and 1960s (Prough, 2011) as postmodernism began to influence narratives and images considerably (Azuma, 2001; Prough, 2011). Reversing gender and sex roles became popular in mass entertainment by the 1970s. The settings included exciting historical places, exotic locales, and even outer space and imaginary places. Before the 1960s, *shojo manga* artists had been only men, with a few female artist assistants (Prough, 2011, p. 46). In the 1970s, a female artist cohort called "Showa 24 [1949]" (based on the imperial Japanese numbering of the birth year of the artist) assumed leadership, invigorated *shojo manga*, and enhanced artistic visualization (pp. 47- 48). Also, in the 1970s, light sexual content was added to satisfy the appetite of an emerging affluent, younger class of entertainment consumers (White 1993).

By the 1980s, *shojo manga* had begun to appeal to adults, the early readers having mostly matured (Prough, 2011, p. 52). The content sometimes dealt with lesbian relationships, the daily life of a career woman, or being a young mother, a housewife, or a widow. In 1975, Waki Yamato, one of the Showa 24 cohort (p. 48), began to write *Haikarasan ga toru* (Here comes Miss Modern), a romantic comedy series comprising 10 books published through 1977. *Haikarasan* told the fictional story of Benio, a boyish 17-year-old schoolgirl in Tokyo *circa* 1920 who grew up to become a journalist, a rare profession for a woman in those days. After initially resisting bridal training to become *ryosaikenbo* (good wife/wise mother), she falls in love with and marries an army officer named Shinobu, a Japanese-German *(hafu)* chosen by both sets of parents before her birth to become her fiancé. When Yamato wrote *Babysitter Gin* in 1998, the heroine she created appealed to the loyal readers of *Haikarasan*. In a way, Yamato virtually brought her readers into the stories as the young mother clients would bring in Gin. Yamato's cross-generational print media work helped build anticipation and unified readers into their imagined community.

Manga Gin was fictional, of course, and magical—not meant to be perceived as real or even possible. Her image was an imaginary replica of an ideal nanny who was transgender. According to Taussig's (1993) notions of *mimesis* and *alterity,* Gin represented an "Other," an *alterity,* someone other than an actual human nanny. Taussig asserts that the mimetic faculty is "the nature that culture uses to create second nature, the faculty to copy, imitate, . . . yield into and become Other" (p. xiii). Gin's image was a commodity discharging more power than actual nannies could in real life, "the magic of mimesis wherein the replication, the copy, acquires the power of the represented" (p. 16). As a result, Appadurai (1996) argues, media technology provides mental and physical activity rather than a respite.

Takuro Ohno's TV performance was based on *manga* Gin, meaning a copy of a copy. Though *manga* readers could imagine Gin in comparison to their mother or grandmother, TV viewers were free to use their imagination however they wanted. These spectators did not need to care about the origin of Gin's performance. What matters is Gin's performance and how that stimulates the spectator's mind, because imagination plays a central role in cultural production and is treated as real (Appadurai, 1996) in postmodern society. The mimesis idea corresponds with Baudrillard's (1976/1993, 1981/1994) idea of the *simulacrum*—neither original nor copy—which pervades late capitalist society. The advance of media technology helped heighten the work of the imagination. The better the *simulacra*, the more stimulating the product. While watching TV and seeking ephemeral pleasure, spectators engage in imagining and flipping back and forth between their knowledge and memory, creating and engaging in socially imagined communities (Appadurai, 1996, pp. 7-8, cited by Akita & Kenney, 2016).

In the postmodern age, a media message or image produced by capitalists may be diffused insidiously, tacitly, and unconsciously to be consumed by the consumers. For example, smartphone users may think they are fully in control, selecting a product and choosing its function for their convenience; however, without knowing, they may become so immersed in the new technology that it begins to partly control or exert influence over their lives. Benjamin (1933/1979; 1982/1999, cited by Akita, 2013) studies the magical power and fantasy energy that emerge from mimesis embedded with commodities and new technologies. The industrial world has become re-enchanted on an unconscious level (Benjamin, 1982/1999). In this respect, I discern production of media messages/images in capitalistic society as a colonial project for capitalists. Hereafter, message/image producers become colonizers—and consumers, the colonized.

To identify colonial devices embedded in *Babysitter Gin* through two different media (*shojo manga* and TV drama) and to uncover the colonial relationship with consumers (readers/spectators), postcolonial thought is helpful and imperative. The postcolonial assumption is that history is a product of colonizers and colonizing. Colonizers are manipulative and self-deceptive. When colonizers try to appeal to the colonized, the colonized are vulnerable and subjected to the colonizers' message/image/gaze. Placed under the dominant force, the colonized may surrender, worship, fantasize about, or imitate the colonizers for survival (Sider, 1987). Despite an initial resistance, the colonized may give in: "Domination even at its most violent can still be permeated with ambiguity, uncertainty, and peculiar mixtures of fantasy and reality; resistance can occur simultaneously with collusion" (p. 3). Thus, culture is produced collaboratively. It is not just a *manga* artist's gender, creative mind, and artistic skills that provide the readers' experience through the art, but also the editor's opinions as well as desires and imagination from the artist's fans and readers/spectators that all collusively and collaboratively work together to create the consumers' experience. Consumers are not just colonized passively; they actively participate through thought and action, such as when trying to dress like a *manga* character.

Among postcolonial theoretical threads, I next apply Bhabha's (1994) ideas of *hybridity, mimicry*, and *ambivalence* to analyze *Babysitter Gin*. Gin's identity, a hybridity of gender, sex, culture, modernity, and tradition, appeals to consumers because Gin is a mimicry of a woman, a nanny, and a good wife/ wise mother. The "magic of mimesis" (Taussig, 1993) has exuded not only a magical fantasy but also alterity: a fetishized representation who we or they are not. Bhabha (1994) asserted, "The discourse of mimicry is constructed around an *ambivalence*; in order to be effective, mimicry must continually produce its slippage, its excess, its difference" (p. 86). *Ambivalence* is embedded in the representation of Gin in TV more implicitly and powerfully.

According to Bhabha (1994), cultural differences confound tradition and modernity in a *hybridity* that can be achieved in borderline engagements: liminal (in-between) and contemporaneous space and temporal moments that may be displaced and decentered. In the *manga*, as a mimicry of Mary Poppins, Gin plays with magic often, which seizes or displaces both characters and readers. Sudden images and nostalgic scenes without many words disorient the characters and readers, keeping them in liminal moments and forcing readers to use their imaginations. Those images speak directly to the hearts of the readers. On the other hand, every TV episode of *Gin* includes a singing-and-dancing flash mob that wins the hearts of spectators, who are mesmerized and induced to dance and sing along with Gin. Readers are captivated by the apparent magic, and spectators are entranced, persuaded, consoled, and invigorated by the dancing and singing of characters. Readers/ spectators are drawn to, displaced, confused by, and enchanted by the magic of their colonizers' borderline engagements.

In postmodern cultural production, a mixture of the traditional and the modern creates fantasy. Taussig (1993) identifies "the surfacing of 'the primitive' within modernity as a direct result of modernity" (p. 20). Mothering is the key to the economic productivity of Japanese capitalism today (Allison, 2000). *Hybridity* of the traditional/modern mother is effective for the colonial project, and it is peppered around *Babysitter Gin*. For instance, Gin recommends breast-feeding (traditional) instead of baby formula and disposable diapers (modern) instead of traditional cloth diapers.

Hybridity subverts the colonial power and the dominant discourse (Bhabha 1994). In colonial discourse, *doubles* are created collaboratively by colonizers and the colonized (Bhabha 1994). Colonizers need these *doubles*, who speak their language and understand their culture. *Gin*, a man in vintage women's attire who aspires to be a mother, desires to have her own baby, and behaves like a woman, is a *double*. The more the *double* is like the original, the more effective the mimicry is, but there must be a slippage, an *ambivalence*, a difference from the original. *Manga* Gin, without any makeup, was depicted as a strong, big-hearted maternalistic nanny. On the other hand, TV Gin wears two social masks. As a nanny, she wears heavy makeup and appears traditionally feminine. However, in the evening, Gin dons a man's business suit and goes to a bar for a drink alone. Each time, Professor Kami-ohka, a 50ish woman who is a self-proclaimed *kosodate mystra* (child-rearing specialist), is there to flirt with Gin, who plays the gentleman, buying her a martini and listening empathetically. TV Gin's *double* is more magically appealing to all types of viewers.

Babysitter Gin deals with topics such as a new mother's struggle to care for her baby alone, a loveless marriage (the baby was conceived not through romantic courtship, but instead during a premarital one-night stand), a new wife's obedience to her mother-in-law, a difficult child, a stage mom, and a teenaged pregnant mom. Though *manga* stories are voluminous, NHK broadcast only ten episodes, and each 50-minute show, except for the pilot, which appeared 20 years earlier, was significantly revised from the original *manga*. The order of the TV episodes was inconsistent with the original *manga* except for the pilot. This demonstrated the TV producers' ardent desire to define Gin's identity and display the framework of the show clearly in the first episode. Goffman (1959) discussed the importance of setting for actors' performance from the dramaturgical perspective. The setting for the first episode of the *Babysitter Gin*'s TV series impresses the audience by defining Gin and her relationship with other characters.

A synopsis and analysis of this first TV episode follows:

Baby Nao is crying profusely as the show begins. At his side, his mother, Kumiko, munches a big chunk of uncooked ramen noodles like a cracker, exposing her poor eating habits, weariness, and self-defeating lifestyle. Kumiko, who alone cares for her newborn, suffers from postpartum depression. Lethargic and exasperated, Kumiko reaches for a flier touting Gin's babysitter agency, mistaking it for a food delivery flier, and dials its phone number. When Gin shows up at the door, Kumiko closes the door on her, saying it was a mistake. Gin barges in and immediately starts taking care of the baby and taking on housework. The baby starts to babble right away. Gin goes to the kitchen and finds a can of powdered baby formula. She scolds Kumiko and advises her to breastfeed. Kumiko confides to Gin about her difficulty secreting milk. Gin suggests that Kumiko's poor diet has prevented her from lactating. Gin cleans up the pantry and removes all the junk food.

Kumiko's breasts start to ache. Gin urgently opens Kumiko's top and starts massaging her breasts like an EMT. Soon, milk shoots up in the air, enabling Kumiko to breastfeed.

Kumiko's husband, Makoto, a typical breadwinner, comes home and immediately heads to the bathroom. Gin storms into the bathroom and gives the baby to the father for bathing. Gin teaches Kumiko how to cook healthy meals, which helps Kumiko to lactate for nursing her newborn. After dinner, Gin directs the couple to clean their house thoroughly for the sake of their baby's hygiene.

Makoto is not interested in taking care of his son. Kumiko is obedient to her husband and his mother and so blames herself for being an insufficient mother and for how the unplanned baby has destroyed the romance in her "shotgun" marriage. Kumiko confesses all of this to Gin, wondering whether the marriage was a mistake.

The next day, Gin transforms Kumiko with a "makeover": a new hairstyle, makeup, and dress. This makeover is intended to fuse the intersecting identities of an attractive woman with a desperate nursing mother. Then, Gin stages a romantic dinner for the couple in a fancy restaurant while Gin babysits Nao. The couple's romantic dinner is disrupted when Makoto takes a call from his mother. That evening, Gin has Kumiko spend the night at Gin's house, while forcing Makoto to take care of the baby alone at home as Gin supervises. Unable to sleep well, Makoto realizes his wife's heavy burden. In the morning, Makoto goes searching for his wife in a park and, from a distance, sees his wife hugging a strange man. He rushes over to confront and strike the man, only to find it was Gin. Now upset with Makoto, Kumiko asks Makoto for a divorce, finally blaming him for their shotgun marriage and her plight. Makoto confesses that it was not a shotgun wedding after all. He swears that he fell in love with Kumiko at first sight at his company's picnic. Kumiko brought *nukazuke* (traditional homemade vegetable pickles) with rice balls, when the other young women brought fancier, more modern dishes, which instantly caused Makoto to develop a crush on her. He methodically planned their first date. This confession saves their marriage. Gin vanishes, and the episode has its happy ending.

Episode One immediately defines Gin's identity as *simulacra* of a woman and mother to the other characters—and virtually, the show's spectators, as well. After seven minutes' background exposing Kumiko as an unhappy and struggling young mother, Gin appears, singing a popular Japanese song, *Konichiwa akachan* ("Hello, my baby"), while walking to her client's house. She arrives at the door upon finishing the line "I am your mother!" Hearing a baby's cry, Gin rushes in. She instructs Kumiko to spread a towel on the floor for the baby's physical exercise. A series of orders about baby care and domestic chores follows. In an attempt to construct a mother through Gin, the colonizers—the show's producers—present *simulacra* of a mother by having her handle a series of chores as a ritual, as they know that "a woman is ensconcing herself in the ritualization . . . of being a mother in Japan" (Allison, 2000, p. 96). Though Allison's research was about a mother's cooking a lunchbox for her family, I argue that in Japan a mother expresses motherhood by performing domestic work, as Gin demonstrated. Gin can make herself an excellent mother, but she is *alterity*, a transgender nanny. Trying to imprint Gin with a mother image, the colonizers have Gin repeat "I am your mother!" throughout the show. In both the *manga* and TV series, Gin, portrayed as a nonsexual average-looking woman, laments her inability to have her own biological baby and attests that she would do anything to make a baby happy. This makes Gin an effective *double*, as it pleases mother-viewers with children, making them feel lucky, proud, and superior to Gin.

The characters in the stories, including Kumiko from Episode One, crave Gin's comforting, motherly hug. Kumiko confides to Gin that her inability to hold her baby properly is because of her own childhood without a mother to hold her. Instantly, Gin holds Kumiko gently, comforting her like a real mother, an emergent identity. That moment, Kumiko and the readers/spectators are transported into Gin's arms and cradled to the hum of a lullaby. The colonizers stage the liminal moments in Gin's arms, knowing that a mother's hug—especially for adults—is unconventional in Japan, but making it seem as if it were nothing unusual. Colonizers take the liberty to write a new history: an "imagined nostalgia" (Appadurai, 1996, p. 77). This makes it possible to create experiences of loss that never took place, thus increasing desire among viewers more. In Episode One, Makoto confesses that Kumiko's *nukazuke* pickles help him realize that she would make an ideal mother according to what the Japanese used to say. Nowadays this is hardly ever heard. The colonizers interjected an "imagined nostalgia" and infused a modern mother with tradition to create an attractive *double* for the audience.

Bhabha (1994, cited by Akita & Kenney, 2016) asserted that an unsolvable binary of sameness and difference—an *ambivalence*—must remain at the core of *mimicry* and that mimicry is a sign of an articulation by the colonized, expressing a portion of the colonizer's self-identity; and, though it can be performed as mockery, delusion, or deception, if performed too well, it could alert the colonizer to a potential menace. In manga/print media, the imagined community was safely guarded by a mostly female gaze; however, in TV, a transnational male gaze joined the colonizer and the colonized. Colonizers needed to fend off the male gaze or any other illicit or voyeuristic gaze upon female characters in the show. Colonizers had to prevent spectators from turning into colonizers. For instance, Gin had to maintain *shojo manga*'s warm, loving, nonsexual mother image.

In the *manga*, upon Kumiko's utterance of pain from her breast inflammation, Gin urgently unbuttons Kumiko's top and closely scrutinizes her breasts as a home doctor would. Gin quickly begins massaging Kumiko's breast, saying, "We cannot waste any drop of mother's nutritious milk for the baby!" In the middle of the massage, while milk spurts from Kumiko's breast, Makoto comes home. In panic, Kumiko tries to explain, but Makoto pays no attention. On the other hand, the TV camera focuses on Gin as she quickly unhooks Kumiko's bra and removes her top without revealing any part of the breast. Colonizers deflected spectators' gaze and minds, turning the emotion of the scene to one of sympathy rather than anything sexual. *Manga* Gin and Kumiko are not sexualized. Instead, Gin's instinct and expert blunt advice confirms her identity as a mother and medical specialist: the intersecting identities. In TV, colonizers consciously hid Kumiko's breasts by directing the gaze to Gin's back and the couch. The only skin revealed was Kumiko's neck and her face in pain. Thus, maintaining *ambivalence* by covering mother's skin and by guiding the gaze, colonizers were able to protect imagined communities.

Interjecting the breast massage scene 11 minutes, 50 seconds into Episode One clearly shows colonizers' eagerness to define Gin as a trustworthy, caring woman, a licensed professional nanny, and a mother to her clients: the intersection of her multiple identities. *Manga* stories included far more sexually suggestive images and scenes than TV episodes, but images were drawn in discreet silhouette or vague lines, which stimulated the imagination of female readers. In a way, colonizers entrust the colonized to use their imagination to reach ecstatic moments in their imagined community. Similar techniques are observed in the story of the high school girl's pregnancy (TV Episode Three/*Manga* Story Nine), and a fully pregnant woman's early labor at home (TV Episode Nine/*Manga* Story 13). The *manga* girl's breasts were blurred, whereas the TV camera's focus away from her breasts deflected spectators' gazes. In the home labor story, *manga* Gin birthed the baby as a midwife would at her client's home. The TV version skipped the labor scene entirely and showed only the post-labor morning, when Gin was bowing to a departing midwife in a white gown, which influenced viewers to imagine that the midwife had been summoned in the middle of the night. The *ambivalence* of a vague outline drawing in the *manga* and skipping the labor scene on TV allowed colonizers to succeed in keeping the mother image as sacred and nonsexual as possible.

In TV, not only the male gaze but also Takuro Ohno's fans' gaze emerged because his fans are young women. Ohno was 31 years old, an actor, and a fashion model with almost 10 years' experience. When *Babysitter Gin* aired in 2019, he quit acting in Japan and was about to move to New York to study English. To satisfy spectators' curiosity about Ohno, colonizers showed off his dancing and singing skills in every episode. In these moments, children were brought in as dancers. Every flash mob started with a different lyric but ended with Gin's solo, "Today, my dream came true, because I am a nanny, a mother to a baby. I want to tell the world, 'I am a mother!'" To respond, the other dancers sang the refrain, "Nanny, Nanny, the best nanny! The real nanny! Nearby nanny!" This refrain lingers in the minds of the audience after the show and further imprints Gin's *alterity* nanny image. The audience does not care whether Gin projects a real Japanese mother. What matters is the *simulacra* of Ohno's performance.

The last two *manga* stories reveal Gin's life history and her first nanny, Mary Marline, with whom Gin attempted to reunite upon beginning study at Oxford in the UK many years later in her adulthood. Gin finds Mary's home but discovers that she has passed away. Gin also discovers that Mary was transgender, and her birth/dead name was Merrill Arthur Marline. That inspires Gin to go to specialize in nanny education at Norland College in the UK. On the other hand, TV Gin focuses on the present without referring to her life history at all. The colonizers cleverly weave current facts about Takuro Ohno's departure for the United States into the last episode. Gin mistakenly thinks she has received an offer to become a nanny for Meghan Markle and tells everyone that she is moving to Buckingham Palace in the UK. However, it turns out that Gin's sister mistook the telephone call. Gin's new client is "Mrs. Melgan England," not "Mrs. Meghan Markle from England." The TV finale flash mob starts in Gin's living room, but one wall opens, giving way for Gin and dancers to go outside the TV studio and onto the street, where passersby, a film director and a delivery man, join in. Some dancers hold miniature airplanes, symbolizing farewell to Gin as well as to Takuro Ohno, to close the loop for Ohno's fans. This last scene is full of hybridities and enchantment.

In the *manga*, the intended colonized were females who desired gender fluidity and welcomed Gin's advice on the female body, baby care, and relationships as an *alterity* different from a typical mother. The fuzzy drawings and vague images enhanced and protected the readers' imagined community. At the same time, Gin performed as a magician or a witch. All these extraordinary elements were necessary for the colonized to actively enjoy their imagined community. On the other hand, the TV colonizers knew that Ohno could not pass as a woman because of spectators who knew of him. Instead, the colonizers revealed Ohno as a heterosexual male in real life but made sure that his *simulacra* as a woman excelled. The performance of *mimicry-simulacra* played the central role, powerfully colonizing the spectators. In the finale, Gin goes to the bar in her nanny dress. There, the child-rearing specialist professor sits. Throughout the show, Gin and the professor disagree and argue about childrearing. In the bar, the professor tells Gin not to sit in a certain chair because it is reserved for the cool guy she sees occasionally—not realizing that all along, that cool guy has been Gin as a man, yet another intersectional identity. Gin thanks the bartender in his male voice. Stunned, the professor wonders whether Gin is the man in question. Gin leaves the bar; the professor is left jealous that Gin is going to work for the British royal family as a nanny in the UK. Thus, the colonizers have concocted the *hybridity* of Gin's male/female voices, the UK/Japan, the nanny/cool guy, *double*, to colonize the spectators successfully.

NOTE

1. As Fredric Jameson (1991) explained, first-stage market capitalism came about in the 1840s with the invention of photography and realism; second-stage monopoly capitalism, in the 1890s with cinema and modernism; then, multinational capitalism in the 1940s with electronic technology. Second-stage monopoly capitalism, in the 1890s with cinema and modernism; then, multinational capitalism in the 1940s with electronic technology. By the 1970s, *late capitalism*, or informational capitalism, pervaded society and deeply impacted the way culture is formed and how we communicate via microelectronics, telecommunications, and computers.

REFERENCES

Akita, K. (2013). Queer male TV commentators: *Kinjo-no-Obasan* in advanced capitalism. In J. Campbell, & T. Carilli (Eds.), *Queer media images: LGBT perspectives* (pp. 89–97). Lexington Book.

Akita, K., & R. Kenney. (2016). Mixing man and monkey in *Planet of the Apes*. In C. Johnson (Ed.), *Tim Burton: Essay on the films* (pp. 102–116). McFarland & Company, Inc.

Allison, A. (2000). *Mothers, comics, and censorship in Japan*. University of California Press.

Anderson, B. (1983). *Imagined communities*: Reflections on the origin and spread of nationalism. Verso.

Appadurai, A. (1996). *Modernity at large: Cultural dimensions of globalization* University of Minnesota Press.

Azuma, H. (2001). *Dobutsuka suru postmodern: Otaku kara mita nihon shakai* [Anthropomorphizing postmodern: Japanese society from *otaku's* perspectives]. Kodansha.

Baudrillard, J. (1993). *Symbolic exchange and death*. London: Sage Publications (Original work published 1976).

Baudrillard, J. (1994). *Simulacra and simulation: The body, in theory*. University of Michigan Press (Original work published 1981).

Benjamin, W. (1979). Doctrine of the similar. (K. Tarnowski, Trans.). *New German critique, 17*, 65–69. (Original work composed in 1933).

Benjamin, W. (1999). *The arcades project.* (R. Tiedemann, Ed.; H. Eiland & K. McLaughlin, Trans). Belknap Press of Harvard University Press. (Original work published 1982, originally composed between 1927 and 1940).

Bhabha, H. (1994). *The location of culture.* Routledge.

Crenshaw, K. W. (1994). Mapping the margins: Intersectionality, identity politics, and violence against women of color. In M. A. Fineman, & R. Mykitiuk (Eds.), *The public nature of private violence* (pp. 93–118). Routledge.

Goffman, E. (1959). *The presentation of self in everyday life.* Doubleday.

Jameson, F. (1991). *Postmodernism, or, the cultural logic of late capitalism.* Duke University Press.

Plath, D. W. (1980). *Long engagements: Maturity in modern Japan.* Stanford University Press.

Prough, J. S. (2011). *Straight from the heart: Gender, intimacy, and the cultural production of shojo manga.* University of Hawaii Press.

Robertson, J. (1998). *Takarazuka: Sexual politics and popular culture in modern Japan.* University of California Press.

Shields, S. A. (2008). Gender: An intersectionality perspective. *Sex Roles, 59*(5–6), 301–311.

Sider, G. (1987). Why parrots learn to talk, and why they can't: Domination, deception, and self-deception in Indian-White relations. *Comparative Study of Society and History, 29*(1), 3–23.

Taussig, M. (1993). *Mimesis and alterity: A particular history of the senses.* Routledge.

White, M. (1993). *The material child: Coming of age in Japan and America.* University of California Press.

Yamato, W. (1998–2007). *Babysitter Gin* (Vol. 1–9). Kodansha Comics Kiss.

Chapter 6

The Intersection of Ethnicity, Gender, and Class in the HBO Series *My Brilliant Friend*

The Cost of Defiance and Resistance

Theresa Carilli

Several years ago on my way to the Italian Canadian Writers' Association conference in Padula, Italy, I stopped for a brief time in Naples to see the location of my grandparents' departure *en route* to America from Sicily, and to see a part of Italy which was mentioned in several family stories. Staying at a boutique hotel bordering the ocean, I proudly introduced myself to the hotel proprietor. Remembering what my father taught me to say, even though I cannot speak Italian, I told the proprietor that I was an Italian American. To my surprise, my disclosure was met with an icy reception. After examining me, she explained that I was American, even if I did not see myself that way. "When did your family leave Italy?" she inquired. "About one hundred years ago," I replied. "You see," she nodded, "Your family has been in America for a long time."

I paused and thought about what seemed like an identity admonishment. Taken aback, I now had to resolve my identity as an Italian American. At 60 years old, this was a challenging task, since I always confirmed the importance and value of my identity both personally and professionally. I grew up in a bilingual household where my parents' shame resulted in their unwillingness to teach my sisters and me the Italian language, and specifically the Sicilian dialect. Friends born in Italy had always validated my ethnic identity and accepted me for my Italian-ness.

When the HBO series *My Brilliant Friend* debuted, I felt a searing longing for the world created and developed by director Saverio Costanzo and written by Elena Ferrante. While there are four books in the series and two

79

HBO seasons released, my focus will be exclusively on the first season, which lays the groundwork for the series. *My Brilliant Friend* is HBO's first non-English-speaking series. As I was pulled back to the motherland, I knew that viscerally I understood this world, a world of two young girls whose friendship was tossed, pulled, destroyed, manipulated, and sabotaged as they attempted to make their ways through their identities as working-class females. Their bond with one another stands as a statement of defiance and resistance. Despite being working class and female, they maintained an allegiance that extended beyond their identities. Defiance and resistance are the worldview and lens through which many working-class women live so they may survive to become productive individuals. For me, this connection with the Italian/Napolitana identity of these two girls/young women added the dimension of cultural sensibility. I know this world. I have lived in it, and I know the effects it has had on me.

In this chapter, I explore that reach back into my ethnic identity and into the cultural sensibility which gives me a specific understanding of this series. I will describe some of the painfully nuanced scenes that examine the intersection between gender, ethnicity/culture, and class in 1950s southern Italy, focusing attention on the limitations this intersection presents to girls and women with a deeper and more hopeful vision of themselves. The suffocating effects of growing up as a working-class female in a patriarchal ethnicity mandate a move toward defiance, and thus, resistance. A working-class Italian or Italian American woman who longs for professional achievement must break through the cultural rules and barriers which keep her contained in a servile, caretaking role. To do this, she must locate unique ways to express herself—to walk that line between seeming rebellious and being acquiescent. This dialectic makes her unique because she takes the strength she has learned as a mother-centered individual (Gambino, 1974) who makes decisions for her family while complying with patriarchal values, ultimately reformulating this identity to become an individual with the ability to think and act independently. That which makes her strong can also make her an anomaly among Italian and Italian American women and create an internal conflict. As a way of mitigating against this acquiescent personality so often depicted as the "mamma" figure in the modern American consciousness, stirring the pasta with a baby in her arms and wearing a black, shapeless dress, her only recourse is to expressively display defiance and resistance. These expressions of defiance and resistance are often highly energized displays so that the Italian and Italian American woman can convince herself, in addition to those around her, that she matters in a world that sees her as invisible. What might seem like anger is a reification and affirmation of self. Before I describe moments of defiance and resistance in *My Brilliant Friend*, I will examine how and why I have been drawn into this intersectional world.

Over the last decade, many DNA services such as *Ancestry, My Heritage,* and *23 and Me* have offered individuals the opportunity to explore their ethnic and racial backgrounds. The popularity of these services points to the simple fact that so many Americans were stripped of their history upon coming to this country. This longing and desire to know about their past has created an industry. While some respond to it skeptically, others, like me, eagerly wish to reach into the past to see how we became Americans and what ethnic and racial remnants have remained with us. In their 2017 article "Delivering the Past: Providing Personalized Ancestral Tourism Experiences," Alexander et al., explore the popularity of ancestral tourism, whereby individuals visit their countries of origin. According to these researchers, the popularity of ancestral tourism has risen as people feel "the pull of a distant homeland" (543) that "allows visitors to experience mediated versions of the past in the present and create individual journeys of self-discovery" (544). Alexander et al. continue, "Traveling to places of personal, religious, cultural, and/or vocational interest may, in certain circumstances, stimulate feelings of nostalgia or deep emotion" (544). This need for a connection to one's country of origin implies some degree of feeling estranged from an unknown entity. Only by experiencing that entity can one come closer to an understanding of where she comes from and who she is. When I stood in the doorways of my grandmothers' homes in Palazzolo, Sicily, I felt a visceral familiarity, even though I had never met either of them. I knew them through my encounters with their homes. Reading a novel or watching a series of novels come to life on screen in the country of an individual's origin creates an opportunity for ancestral tourism. In the case of *My Brilliant Friend*, spectators enter post–World War II Naples during the 1950s. Many southern Italians left for America from the port of Naples, including my grandparents. When I entered this visual world, it was as though my memory was being jogged, and I could reach back into my ancestors' histories.

In his 1986 article "Ethnicity and the Post-Modern Arts of Memory," Michael Fischer examines autobiographical literature, which has ethnicity as a key focus. Fischer reaches three major conclusions about ethnicity, after studying Maxine Hong Kingston's *The Woman Warrior* (1976), Michael Arlen's *Passage to Ararat* (1975), and Marita Golden's *Migrations of the Heart* (1983). According to Fischer:

> Ethnicity is not something that is simply passed on from generation to generation, taught and learned; it is something dynamic, often unsuccessfully repressed or avoided. . . . Insofar as ethnicity is a deeply rooted emotional component of identity, it is often transmitted less through cognitive language or learning (to which sociology has almost entirely restricted itself) than through

processes analogous to the dreaming and transference of psychoanalytical encounters. (195)

Fischer explores the idea that being a "hyphenated American," such as a Chinese-American, requires locating a new voice by integrating a "pluralist, multidimensional, or multi-faceted concept of self" (197). Finally, he acknowledges that the process of struggling with ethnic identity is a form of discovery that can develop into new methods for the study of identity.

By connecting back to ancestral memory, Fischer believes individuals can understand their ethnic identities while inventing new identities that are culturally based. Based on the Jungian theory of the collective unconscious, ancestral memory invites individuals to delve into those memories which begin with individuals' connections with particular cultures, whether those cultures are their countries of origin or a culture with which they feel a deep connection. This tie to ancestral memory means forging ethnic and cultural identity through self-exploration, self-discovery, and self-realization.

In his blog, "Ancestral or Genetic Memory: Factory Installed Software," Darold Treffert examines why prodigious savants exist. Treffert delves into ancestral memory, terming it, "genetic memory." Genetic memory, according to Treffert, is a third type of memory, after cognitive/semantic memory and procedural/habit memory, the two most commonly accepted types of memory. According to Treffert:

> It is generally accepted that we can inherit certain physical characteristics such as height, weight, hair color, eye color, and even propensity to certain diseases, for example. It is also generally accepted that certain behavioral traits, or even talents, can "run in families" and we see evidence of that all around us. Genetic memory simply adds bits of inherited knowledge to that passed on mix of genes, chromosomes and cells instead of settling for the view that we start our lives with completely blank memory or knowledge disks to which we add only those life experiences and learning that occur after we are born.

Treffert explains that savants were given their knowledge and skills through genetic transmission. While Treffert asserts that genetic memory is primarily biological, it has a transpersonal component. If individuals inherit the knowledge of their ancestors, possibly they inherit the consciousness of their ancestors. Thus, genetic and transpersonal knowledge are parts of their makeup that might formulate their worldviews.

When I first watched the HBO show *My Brilliant Friend*, I felt magically transported to a familiar time and place and into a world that I understood with stunning clarity. In the next section of this chapter, I will give a history of this series and propose a framework for studying intersectionality.

Focusing on ethnicity/culture, gender, and class, I will explore how the series captures Naples and how it has spoken to me in a way that allowed for both healing and a better understanding of my background.

My Brilliant Friend is based on the first book of the Neapolitan novels written by Elena Ferrante. Ferrante has assumed a pseudonym for this series, perhaps for several reasons. An Italian journalist, Claudio Gatti, believes that Ferrante is Anita Raja, a translator who lives in Rome. By following Raja's financial success, Gatti believes the author of this series is Raja. In a *New York Times* article by Alexandra Schwartz, Gatti exposes why Ferrante has remained anonymous:

> Ferrante mentions that Italo Calvino told a scholar of his work that he might answer questions put to him, but not with the truth. In a letter to her publisher, she writes that if pressured, she may occasionally resort to telling lies about herself "to shield my person, feelings, pressures."

While Raja has never admitted to being Ferrante, readers perhaps can speculate why the author remains hidden. With searing honesty, the writer explores the coming-of-age of two female friends who travel through their lives being haunted and challenged by their class backgrounds, their gender, and the Italian cultural value of "omerta." According to Theresa Carilli (2005), *Omerta* (the code of silence) has roots in Sicilian history; various countries invaded Sicily and attempted to infiltrate and overthrow its government. As a protective measure, Sicilians learned to keep silent and created a familial government so that allegiance was only to other Sicilians and to the family.

Naples, like Sicily, is in the southern part of Italy, following many of the same cultural rules. In 1985, Helen Barolini explored the absence of Italian American writers, an absence she attributed to omerta. In 1999, literary critic Mary Jo Bona explained that Italian American writers were beginning to break the code of silence by introducing stories that rendered the Italian American family:

> Omerta—has peculiar resonance for women of Italian origins and for women who want to write. Perhaps the codes informing the southern Italian family were considered inviolate in Italy, but they were subject to an authority closer to home in America: the wife, the mother, the sister, the daughter. That Italian American writers have chosen to use their family as the focus of their novels, to write of the family and tell its secrets, is a profoundly courageous act of autonomy. (p. 14)

While Barolini and Bona focus their work on Italian Americans, Italian cultural rules and values have been embedded into the consciousness of the daughters and sons of Italians. Writing about family from a cultural perspective, particularly writings by Italian and Italian American women is, as Bona claims, a "courageous" act as well as an act of defiance and resistance. Again, I speculate that Raja/Ferrante suffers from this mixed feeling of bravery and shame, one that I am certain so many Italian American women writers suffer.

The description of Ferrante's novels focuses on a variety of themes. According to journalist Judith Thurman:

> Ferrante's novels are rooted in the notion that primal attachments shape the way that human beings dominate and submit to one another . . . she gives that premise a vivid embodiment in the hostile love—empowering and subversive, jealous and reverent, steadfast and treacherous—between two friends whom we meet as girls of eight, in the slum where they were born, and follow for six decades, through the upheavals of postwar Italian society. Elena Greco and Raffaella Cerullo seem fated from the outset to become their mothers—weary drudges brutalized by their men, who wreak that violence on their daughters, if not by blows then by disparagement. In that respect, each of them has been invisible to herself until her friend gives her the gift of being seen. (p. 5)

Elisa Leonelli describes Ferrante's work as "a fierce criticism of the male-chauvinistic behavior of fathers and husbands, who keep these women oppressed to the point of domestic abuse, and highlight the class conflict between the workers . . . and the bosses" (p. 2).

Other journalists and reviewers focus on the television series as a secret world of female friendship. The characters, Elena Greco (Lenu) and Rafaella Cerullo (Lila) share an intimate bond in their connections with words. Words take them out of their poverty and the limits imposed by their gender identity. Words shape their future hopes and are the secret that binds them in their lifelong friendship. Molly Fischer writes, "They have a shared feeling for language that separates them from the other children in their neighborhood" (p. 3).

In the first season of the series, director Saverio Costanzo takes his audience into 1950s postwar Naples—into a bleak working-class neighborhood where the gray, concrete buildings which resemble American tenement housing are devoid of grass, plants, and spirit. This stark, desolate neighborhood embodies the worldview of its inhabitants. We are introduced to the community families and thrown into their painful worlds. We learn about the dynamics of the community from two young schoolgirls, Lenu (Elisa Del Genio) and Lila (Ludovica Nasti), who are present for the first two episodes of *My Brilliant Friend* and then re-cast by their 14-year-old counterparts, Lenu (Margherita Mazzucco) and Lila (Gaia Girace). In the first grade, Lenu becomes intrigued with Lila, who demonstrates that she can read and write, unlike the other children her age. The competition and love between these two friends emerge in the first episode, "The Dolls." As a way of demonstrating their friendship, Lila and Lenu swap dolls. Then, Lila throws Lenu's doll into a basement, sparking Lenu to do the same. Lenu says to Lila, "What you do, I do." At this point, we hear the narrator (Alba Rohrwacher) speak: "We always felt we were going to run into something terrible, which even though it had existed before us had always been waiting for us" (Ferrante et al., 2018a). This fatalistic statement underlines the pain and desperation of growing up in a community where females have few options. The girls try to retrieve the dolls from a notoriously criminal neighbor, Don Achille Carracci (Antonio Pennarella), who gives them some money in place of helping them to locate the dolls. Eventually, Don Achille is killed, and we learn later that he would have been Lila's future father-in-law. In the second episode, "The Money," the girls take the money Don Achille has given them and hide it until they find the appropriate time to retrieve it and purchase a copy of *Little Women*. After reading the book several times, they give it away when it becomes clear that Lila's parents will not allow her to enter middle school, believing she has all the education a girl needs.

Lila encourages Lenu to accompany her to the ocean, a place they have never been. To explain their day-long absence, the girls tell their parents that their teacher is hosting a party they plan on attending. As Lenu and Lila walk outside of their neighborhood, the audience experiences the terror and joy of being outside the realm of familiarity, though the girls have only temporarily freed themselves because they never make it to the ocean. Sadly defeated, they return to their suburban Naples community in the rain. Lenu sees her mother, who is anxiously looking for her. She decides to face the consequences and walks up to her mother, who hits her with an umbrella, yelling, "I'll kill you, you wretched girl. Wait till I tell your father." Lenu's mother, Immacolata Greco (Annarita Vitolo), brings her home and beats her while saying to her husband, "You have to beat her too." When Lenu's father, Vittorio Greco (Luca Gallone), hesitates, Immacolata speaks angrily, "You don't even know how to hit your daughter! What kind of man are you?" (Ferrante et al., 2018b). At this point, Vittorio beats his daughter until Immacolata stops him. Moments later, the viewers see Lenu back in school with her face badly bruised. Lenu's parents have just enacted a father-dominated, mother-centered familial relationship, whereby the mother tells the father how to perform his role as a man and a father so she can maintain control over the family.

Later we watch young Lila getting thrown from the balcony of her apartment by her father, Fernando Cerullo (Antonio Buonanno), who refuses to allow Lila to continue her schooling. "You'll do what I say because I'm your father," he screams (Ferrante et al., 2018b). As Lenu approaches Lila on the ground, Lila insists she is not in any pain, contradicting what the audience sees.

In the third episode, we meet teenaged Lenu and Lila. Lenu has been grieving over the loss of seeing her friend in school, while Lila has begun to work with her brother Rino (Gennaro De Stefano) in the family business. Lila begins designing shoes for the business, demonstrating both her creative talent and the strength of her character. In this episode, Lenu's teacher, Miss Oliviero (Dora Romano), visits Lenua's family:

Miss Oliviero (to Lenu): So it's decided you're going to high school, but you've got to be the best in school or it will be trouble. (Miss Oliviero departs.)

Immacolata: (to Lenu) Damn you and that f-----g school. We can't say no, or she'll (Miss Oliviero) take it out on Elisa (another daughter). That Oliviero woman pisses me off. She gets these ideas and then we have to make sacrifices.

Vittorio: (to Lenu) I'll break your legs if I see you with (a neighborhood boy). I'll break your legs one at a time.

Immacolata: (to Lenu) I can't believe you'll still be going to school. You make me curse God. (Ferrante et al., 2018c)

Despite the emotional and physical abuse both girls suffer at their parents' hands, they remain spirited and connected to one another. This connection results from their intellectual curiosity and determination to understand and live in a world outside of suburban Naples. The girls nurture one another when no one else does. Lenu appears as "the good girl" while Lila is seen as the "troubled one." Lila teaches Lenu to understand and speak Latin and later, Greek, languages which represent upward mobility. She encourages Lenu in her education, knowing that Lenu will one day be her opportunity to move outside the small-minded patriarchal world the girls inhabit. As working-class girls, Lenu and Lila demonstrate resistance with their dogged determination to become educated. When Lila is no longer allowed to attend school, she secretly frequents the library, where she reads voraciously. While Lenu's parents react negatively to their daughter becoming educated, the determined Lenu does not quit. Quietly, she pursues the dream of being educated. Being educated becomes a way of changing one's circumstances.

During the next few episodes of the first season, we are introduced to the Solaras, Marcello (Elvis Esposito), and Michele (Alessio Gallo), They are the embodiment of class struggle. The Solaras, who demonstrate their male and class privilege, are introduced to the audience as they invite a neighborhood girl, Ada Cappuccio (Ulrike Migliaresi), into their new car, signaling their intention to rape a female from a lower class. Lila condemns this action to the other neighborhood girls, explaining that the Solaras are "abducting" Ada (Ferrante et al., 2018c):

Lila (to Lenu): I'm busy. If you wanna waste time watching the Solaras and you're happy with how they treat you, go right ahead. But I have to work. I have to make money . . . Just look at how the Solaras behave. Pinuccia Carracci, who's beautiful, they've never bothered her. You know why they act like this with Ada?
Lenu: No.
Lila: Because she's poor. She doesn't count. To escape this neighborhood, you need money and to make money, you need work that pays. (pause) They don't touch me because I'm ugly. But if it happens, until I get richer, I'll defend myself with this. (Lila shows her knife to Lenu.)

In this interaction between Lila and Lenu, Lila attempts to explain to Lenu how they are both at a disadvantage as working-class females in their community. Throughout the season, Lila imparts her wisdom to Lenu. Later, Marcello attempts to get Lila into his car, and she brandishes the knife, threatening to use it on him. After Lila accidentally dances with Marcello at a party, he begins visiting her family and makes his intentions to marry Lila known to her father, Fernando. Lila's family is excited about this prospect, seeing this as an opportunity to change their class status. Even though Marcello represents the rich, criminal underbelly of this Napolitano community, he also represents one way out. In the following interaction (Ferrante et al., 2018d), Lila's parents attempt to convince her to marry Marcello:

Fernando (Lila's father): You don't have to give an answer right away. But I'd advise you to say yes, not just for you but for the whole family.
Nunzio (Valentina Acca, Lila's mother): That's right. We need to think about your life, but about us, too. Marcello Solara is a good boy. He treats your father with respect.
Fernando: You only have to say yes, and I'll take care of the rest. We'll take it step by step. Understand?
Lila: Are you asking me if I understand or if I want to?
Fernando: Both.
Lila: Papa, rather than marrying Marcello Solara, I'd rather jump in the swamp!
Father: You'll do as I say.
Lila: No. (Fernando slaps her across the face.)
Lila: Not even if you kill me.

Much like Lenu's parents, who chastise her for going to school and committing a "selfish" act, Lila's parents encourage the marriage between Marcello and Lila for their benefit. They treat Lila as being "selfish," communal property who defies them, making decisions for her life, instead of her family's life. Once again, Lila's gender and class background intersect, as she is not encouraged to make independent decisions. Her defiance and resistance are brave acts that could separate her from the family. Lila shuns Marcello, despite his numerous efforts to win her over. Eventually, she commits to Stefano Carracci (Giovanni Amura), Don Achille's oldest son. Initially, Lila seems content with Stefano because she trusts him, unlike Marcello. When, however, Stefano learns that because the Cerullo shoe business cannot make a substantial profit selling shoes, Stefano plans to build a shoe empire with the Solaras. The Solaras financially back the business, and Stefano attempts to keep this a secret from Lila, who sees her family shoe business as an artistic enterprise. Between Lila's ability to design shoes and the Solaras' ability to make capital investments, Stefano combines the two worlds, hoping to add to his own personal wealth.

Meanwhile, Lenu has returned from being a caretaker for tourists in the beautiful seaside village of Ischia on the Amalfi coast. Initially thrilled to have achieved her dream of swimming in the ocean, 15-year-old Lenu is now scared and confused, trying to understand the meaning behind being assaulted in Ischia by Donato Sarratore (Emanuele Valenti), a poet, former neighbor, and father of Lenu's classmate, Nino (Francesco Serpico). Donato has a reputation for affairs, particularly with a townswoman named Melina (Pina De Gennaro), who seems to have become crazy as a result of her encounters with him. To ward off Donato's stalking of her, Lenu begins dating a working-class neighborhood boy, Antonio Cappuccio (Christian Giroso), though she has a crush on Sarratore's son, Nino.

Lila gets engaged to Stefano, who promises that Marcello will not be allowed at their wedding. He expresses his love and commitment to her. Lenu demonstrates her support for Lila, encouraging her to speak with Stefano, even though she doubts Stefano's word. Prior to the wedding, Lila makes a promise to Lenu to help her financially with education. When Marcello appears at the wedding, Lila knows she has been betrayed by Stefano and that her instincts were correct. We witness her anger as she is now trapped in this patriarchal world. Instead of finding a way out, Lila has been betrayed by her circumstances.

The intersectional elements of ethnicity, gender, and class drive the plot of *My Brilliant Friend*. This is a world where girls have no future except as housekeepers, wives, mothers, and servants. Following the rules of being a working-class Italian female implies accepting these rules. I learned about these same expectations as a young girl, who like Lenu and Lila, longed to be educated. While my parents entertained the notion of education for me, they seemed to indicate that it was as important as belonging to a club. Although my mother nurtured my childhood imagination by taking me to museums and purchasing any book I requested, she also expressed the cultural ambivalence toward education. A Sicilian saying explains this ambivalence: "Never make your children better than yourself" (Rolle, 1980). I was taught to be humble and servile and to put educational aspirations out of my purview. When I became a professor and writer, I felt haunted by familial messages given to me as a working-class girl. *My Brilliant Friend* has tremendous resonance for me. I strongly identify with both main characters who are attempting to change their lives and worldviews. Through the elements of cultural dynamics and aesthetics, *My Brilliant Friend* conveys the agony of this intersectional identity.

The cultural dynamics demonstrate how girls and women are considered invisible, and how they are beasts of burden. The physical and emotional violence girls and women experience in this cultural world underscore how their existence is of no value. There is never a moment where either main character is given support or self-worth. Even when their teacher, Miss Oliviero, attempts to be supportive, she is tough and unrelenting. At Lila's wedding, Lenu finally understands that she herself is a "plebian," a term that Miss Oliviero tried to teach her. A commoner and a female are dark and unforgiving identities. Surviving in this world requires defiance and resistance. To defy or resist entails fighting, and fighting contradicts the essence of being a passive female. In *My Brilliant Friend*, the audience witnesses defiance in small acts that range from throwing each other's dolls into a basement, symbolic of resisting female identity, and trying to escape to the ocean, a symbol of freedom. Lila's unwillingness to marry the richest man in the neighborhood because of who he is and what he represents, and to belie her parents by educating herself, are acts of defiance and resistance. She never acquiesces, which causes her great pain, but she makes choices to benefit herself. Like all female members of this community, Lila suffers, but she suffers out loud as a way of disrupting a cultural dynamic that keeps females in oppressive situations.

Saverio Costanzo's marvelous direction demonstrates his understanding of this intersection of ethnicity/culture, class, and gender. His aesthetic choices demonstrate the struggles of this Napolitano neighborhood where everyone has limited hopes and expectations. Costanzo selected unknown actors and actresses from Naples who create an authentic feel for what it means to be Italian. These actors and actresses, in turn, capture the struggles of their characters. This solid choice greatly influences how conflicts are expressed. With these performers, their understanding of what it means to be Italian allows the audience to experience the characters' lives. The bleak neighborhood emphasizes the hopelessness and sorrow the characters experience on a day-to-day basis. While there are parties and a wedding where characters appear spirited and lively, scenes are underscored by a fatalistic sensibility that everything will eventually turn into tragedy. Costanzo captures this sensibility through the narrator's observation, "We always felt we were going to run into something terrible which even though it had existed before us had always been waiting for us" (Ferrante et al., 2018a).

For me, this haunting yet familiar feeling captured in *My Brilliant Friend* transports me through my years of pain and through my fight to be separated from the pain that follows me. I could not stop watching *My Brilliant Friend* as I relived every memory of my youth where I was taught the importance of my ethnic identity and where I learned that being female and working class would be guiding markers throughout my life. This intersectionality has taught me to reflect on the high cost of breaking out of one's circumstances— and that resistance and defiance are necessary to accomplish this break. *My Brilliant Friend* allows Italian and Italian American women the opportunity to viscerally reflect on their identities through the visual experience of being transported to a world that lives in our ancestral memories.

REFERENCES

Alexander, M., Bryce, D., & Murdy, S. (2017). Delivering the past: Providing personalized ancestral tourism experiences. *Journal of Travel Research. 56*(4), 543–555.

Barolini, H. (Ed.). (1985). *The dream book: An anthology of writings by Italian American Women.* Schocken.

Bona, M. J. (1999). *Claiming a tradition: Italian American women writers.* Southern Illinois University Press.

Ferrante, E. (2012). *My brilliant friend.* Europa Editions.

Ferrante, E., Piccolo, F., Paolucci, L. (Writers), & Costanzo, S. (Writer & Director). (2018, November 18). Le Bambole (Season 1, Episode 1) [Television series episode]. In F. Rossi & S. Corbucci (Producers), *My brilliant friend.* HBO and RAI Fiction.

Ferrante, E., Piccolo, F., Paolucci, L. (Writers), & Costanzo, S. (Writer & Director). (2018, November 19). I soldi (Season 1, Episode 2) [Television series episode]. In F. Rossi & S. Corbucci (Producers), *My brilliant friend.* HBO and RAI Fiction.

Ferrante, E., Piccolo, F., Paolucci, L. (Writers), & Costanzo, S. (Writer & Director). (2018, November 25). Le metamorfosi (Season 1, Episode 3) [Television series episode]. In F. Rossi & S. Corbucci (Producers), *My brilliant friend.* HBO and RAI Fiction.

Ferrante, E., Piccolo, F., Paolucci, L. (Writers), & Costanzo, S. (Writer & Director). (2018, December 2). Le scarpe (Season 1, Episode 5) [Television series episode]. In F. Rossi & S. Corbucci (Producers), *My brilliant friend.* HBO and RAI Fiction.

Fischer, M. (2014, September 4). *Elena Ferrante and the force of female friendships.* The New Yorker. Retrieved September 4, 2020, from https://www.newyorker.com /books/page-turner/elena-ferrante-liking-like

Fischer, M. J. (1986). Ethnicity and the post-modern arts of memory. In J. Clifford and G. Marcus (Eds.), *Writing culture: The poetics and politics of ethnography.* University of California Press.

Gambino, R. (1974). *Blood of my blood.* Doubleday and Co., Inc.

Leonelli, E. (2020, April 15). *"My Brilliant Friend": From Naples to the world. Television* Entertainment News. Retrieved August 4, 2020, from https://elisaleonell icareer.wordpress.com/2020/04/16/my-brilliant-friend-on-hbo

Rolle, A. (1980). *The Italian Americans: Troubled roots.* University of Oklahoma Press.

Rossi, F. & Corbucci, C (Producers), Costanzo, S. (Director). 2018. My brilliant friend. [TV Series]. HBO and RAI Fiction.

Schwartz, A. (2016, October 3). *The "unmasking" of Elena Ferrante.* The New Yorker. Retrieved September 4, 2020, from https://www.newyorker.com/culture/c ultural-comment/the-unmasking-of-elena-ferrante

Thurman, J. (2020, August 31). *What brings Elena Ferrante's worlds to life.* The New Yorker. Retrieved August 7, 2020, from https://www.newyorker.com/maga zine/2020/08/31/what-brings-elena-ferrantes-worlds-to-life

Treffert, D. (April 25, 2017). *'Ancestral' or 'genetic' memory: Factory installed software.* Agnesian HealthCare. Retrieved August 9, 2020, from https://www.agnesian .com/blog/ancestral-or-genetic-memory-factory-installed-software

Chapter 7

UpWord Mobility

The Intersection of Rhetorics, Hip-Hop, and History in Hamilton: An American Musical

Sara Raffel and Amanda Hill

Hamilton: An American Musical tells the story of Alexander Hamilton, the United States' first treasury secretary. Before the musical's Broadway opening in 2015, Hamilton's contributions to the founding of the country's government and his creation of the federal banking system were often relegated to the margins of textbooks. Like many of our founding fathers, positioned throughout time by whitewashed history as a "great man," Hamilton was the monochromatic figure of 200 years past and a name that graced some public buildings. The musical, however, written by Lin-Manuel Miranda, does not introduce Hamilton as an accomplished scholar, a career politician, and a decorated war veteran. Rather, Miranda's libretto opens with three unlikely adjectives for this vaunted historical figure: "bastard," "orphan," and "son of a whore" (Miranda & McCarter, 2016, p. 15). *Hamilton: An American Musical* (referred to as simply *Hamilton* going forward) thus challenges the visibility and reading of the traditional narrative of our country's forefathers by reimagining Hamilton and his contemporaries not as "great men," but rather as "everymen." The characterization makes Hamilton more relatable to working-class people; he was an immigrant, a tireless worker, a loving though cheating husband. In recognizing and centralizing Hamilton's humanity and passion, the musical shows justice and recognition for oft marginalized cultures in the United States, where the authority presumed by the identity "forefather" distances working-class people from traditional narratives. This "new" narrative of Hamilton's life is told for the people through a people's medium: hip-hop.

By combining hip-hop poetics with American history and musical theater, Hamilton recognizes the importance of marginalized rhetoric. Postmodern and hip-hop scholar Russell A. Potter (1995) writes, "African-American cultures have mobilized, via a network of localized sites and nomadic incursions, cultures of the found, the revalued, the used" (p. 108). Miranda carries this tradition forward, sampling from myriad sources like historical archives written by and about Alexander Hamilton, Ron Chernow's contemporary biography, classic hip-hop styles, and musical theater structures. Miranda seamlessly integrates and celebrates many voices, breaking down hierarchies of rhetoric that value "academic" over "street" vernacular. In *Hamilton*, this chapter argues, the poetics tell a broader narrative than the mere facts of Alexander Hamilton's life; by combining elements of diverse cultures, the musical further highlights the themes of marginalization and resistance already present in American history. The musical thus dramatizes the intersections of race, class, rhetoric, hip-hop, and history, creating a new identity for marginalized individuals.

Using scholarships of rhetoric, hip-hop, and postmodernism, this chapter discusses the musical and its creator Lin-Manuel Miranda as part of hip-hop and remix culture. The authors argue that the musical's hip-hop poetics are a means of transcultural storytelling. The words represent an effort to expose the ways diverse rhetoric opens new channels of visualization and meaning making in dominant historical narratives within changing political and cultural norms. As scholar Tricia Rose (1994) suggests, we thus "imagine these Hip-hop principles as a blueprint for social resistance and affirmation: [to] create sustaining narratives, accumulate them, layer, embellish, and transform them" (p. 39). Revising Alexander Hamilton's narrative using hip-hop poetics transforms him from "founding father" to "bastard" and back again, refiguring his life and place in American history by introducing humanity into its retelling.

Hamilton reminds us that history, like the text, can be participatory, intersectional, and liberating. By remixing America's founding fathers alongside hip-hop's founding fathers, a mixture of modern vernacular and hip-hop rhetoric makes the language and feel of *Hamilton* accessible to diverse ethnic groups who traditionally feel marginalized or pushed away from history created by and for white America, thus reclaiming history for countless Americans in a way that is relatable, fun, and educational. In so doing, *Hamilton* challenges the dominant historical narrative while presenting a fictionalized version of history. The perspective from which Miranda tells the story moves against the traditional vaunted retelling of our forefathers, humanizing them in a way that positions them as ordinary rather than great.

Javon Johnson (2017) discusses the power of the dead in the role of hip-hop and slam culture, which proves illuminating for a discussion of Miranda's musical. Quoting Sharon Patricia Holland's (2000) discussion of

Toni Morrison's *Beloved* in which she claims that the novel allowed the dead to speak, Johnson argues,

> By "raising the dead," black artists have not only disturbed the so-called finite boundaries of the dead and the living but also given rise to the possibilities of unsettling those in/of the margin and center as well as "the static categories of black/white, oppressor/oppressed, [thus] creating a plethora of tensions within and without existing cultures." (p. 18)

Miranda raises the dead in *Hamilton*. He does so by revising the life story of Alexander Hamilton and key political players of Hamilton's time. The ability to "seek the help of the dead to disturb and reject existing boundaries and borders and to imagine new possibilities in the current modes of living" (Johnson, 2017, p. 18) is one seen clearly in the work of Miranda's musical. Indeed, as Tricia Rose points out, "creative fantasies, perspectives, and experiences of racial marginality in America" are part of the ambiance rappers create with their works (1994, p. 3). Miranda invites Hamilton and his compatriots from the land of the dead into the land of the living to "disturb and reject existing boundaries" in an effort to showcase Hamilton as the everyman in a way that serves as "a catalyst for thinking about and working toward spaces and modes of living beyond our existing systems and structures" (Johnson, 2017, p. 19). Johnson writes that in spoken word poetry "death is the beginning of another possibility, something beyond rather than an end" (2017, p. 13). Johnson goes on to suggest that imagining beyond in this artistic way competes with hegemonic structures: "To rethink the boundaries is to leave the problematic system intact, but imagining beyond is an attempt to leave the problematic system altogether" (2017, p. 14). Miranda's *Hamilton* is, arguably, an act of imagining beyond, an attempt to break through the problematic scaffolding that has held history and theater intact for many years.

Miranda's use of remixing and hip-hop to retell a history most often told through the perspectives and vernacular of white men imagines a world beyond these prior narratives. The world that creates these prior narratives is predicated on the available archival and research materials relating to the characters and events. Miranda's research into the life of Alexander Hamilton was extensive, and it is perhaps safe to say that most work he encountered fed the narrative of Hamilton as a "great man" engaged in life-altering events. But even within these works, Miranda saw the everyman Hamilton was. As Thomas Postlewait (1991) reminds us "even the best kinds of written and material evidence—official testimony, a photograph, an object, a building—are not the event . . .Their meanings are potential rather than received" (p. 160). That meanings of archival documents, standard icons of historical truth, can be manipulated, makes space for Miranda to engage in the kinds of imagining beyond what Johnson described. In fact, there is often a space between historical accuracy and narrative development in historical fiction, and *Hamilton* is no exception. The complete minute-to-minute history of these events is unavailable, and recreating this narrative with exact historical accuracy is an unattainable goal, as such. The documentation that remains about the characters and events in this work was created and preserved from those in positions of power and with the understanding that Hamilton himself was a man of power and importance, and therefore "Archives—as records—wield power over the shape and direction of historical scholarship, collective memory, and national identity, over how we know ourselves as individuals, groups, and societies" (Schwartz & Cook, 2002, p. 2). It is partly the power that has been transferred to the maintenance of Alexander Hamilton's archives that position him to maintain his status as a "great man." In recreating Hamilton's narrative for the purpose of art, Miranda chose what to include, what to omit (which has caused significant criticism [Monteiro, 2016; Isenberg, 2016; Goodman, 2020]) and what to imagine beyond. Thus, Miranda serves as a biographer of Hamilton's life with a vastly different interpretation of the man than has previously been employed because he selects and "forgets" the information that he feels makes for a cohesive and engaging narrative (Miranda & McCarter, 2016, p. 82).

Though Miranda plays with the details of the nation's origin story to create a dramatic narrative arc, part of *Hamilton*'s ideology and political contestation also stems from the musical forms Miranda chooses; hip-hop and rap comprise much of the musical score. From a rhetorical standpoint, these poetic forms situate *Hamilton* as a type of counterculture. They are contrary to the typical structure of the musical because of the faster pace of the words; the themes of legacy, hustle, and "representin'" and the multitude of references to classic hip-hop. However, it bears noting that Miranda includes songs in a more traditionally musical theater style, such as the three numbers sung by the King George character: "You'll Be Back" (Miranda & McCarter, 2016, p. 57), "What Comes Next" (Miranda & McCarter, 2016, p. 127), and "I Know Him" (Miranda & McCarter, 2016, p. 218). These songs contrast to the hip-hop songs both in rhetoric and staging. Set with only a single performer on stage, the King George interludes make the punctuated poetry of the rap numbers, such as the two "Cabinet battle" songs (Miranda & McCarter, 2016, pp. 161; 192), stand out as even more revolutionary.

In his book *Gettin' Our Groove On: Rhetoric, Literacy, and Language for the Hip-hop Generation*, Kermit Ernest Campbell asserts "the verbal art of *rappin'* as definitive of rhetoric in the African American vernacular" (2005, p. 23–24), and the Cabinet battle songs are staged in the play as freestyle rap battles, one of the traditional vehicles of hip-hop poetics. In Miranda's retelling, Madison plays the role of "hype man," introducing and setting up

Jefferson's argument against Hamilton. The speaking characters pass around a prop microphone as they exchange words, and the ensemble gathers around them, hanging on each turn of phrase (Miranda & McCarter, 2016, p. 161). The words in these particular songs are the centerpiece, and to acknowledge rap as part of African American vernacular, as Campbell does, is important in this context, given the musical's casting of people of color in the main roles. In Miranda and McCarter's annotated libretto Daveed Diggs, who portrayed Jefferson in the original cast, recalls performing the rap battles for a group of youth from New York City's high schools. The teens were already familiar with the rules of the rap battle that, contrary to traditional theater, encourage audience feedback, and so they:

> felt empowered to let the competing rappers know what they thought. As Hamilton and Jefferson traded arguments (and insults), the actors heard a lot of *OHHHHHs* and cheers. Daveed loves to perform for audiences that don't know the rules but says that it was painful to play Jefferson in the Cabinet battle that day: "They're so vocal, it hurts so much more when I lose." (Miranda & McCarter, 2016, p. 157)

However, one must view the rhetoric as not solely part of a longstanding black tradition but also as a tradition of resistance, as Smitherman (1997) does when she writes: "rap music is not only a Black expressive cultural phenomenon; it is, at the same time, a resisting discourse, a set of communicative practices that constitute a text of resistance against White America's racism and its Euro-centric cultural dominance" (p. 7). Taken in this context, *Hamilton* catalogs the resistance that brought about the American Revolution and liberated the country from English rule while using a discourse of resistance against the white cultural practices that remain powerful today, and in doing so it captures audiences who may have felt marginalized by traditional theater. At the same time, it is cost-prohibitive for those audiences to see the show live, though a fairly comprehensive cast album and 2020 Disney+ release of the original Broadway cast movie help to alleviate that discrepancy. Sammy Alim writes on the relationship between language and race, stating:

> Whites exercise power through overt and covert racist practices, which often reveal racist ideologies that even the 'racist' may be unaware of. . . . In our case, [White Mainstream English] and White ways of speaking become the invisible—or rather inaudible—and unmarked norms of what becomes glassed as "communicating in academic settings." (p. 56)

Hamilton amplifies black vernacular in a manner not previously seen on Broadway, and in doing so calls attention to the dearth of black vernacular in the theater generally. That said, much of *Hamilton*'s strength and appeal stems from the fact that Miranda adeptly pays tribute to two of hip-hop's rhetorical staples: freestyle and remix.

Hamilton is painstakingly written and rehearsed, but several of the musical numbers, like the previously mentioned Cabinet battles and "Farmer Refuted" (Miranda & McCarter, 2016, p. 49), recall Miranda's roots as a freestyle poet. Anthony Veneziale and Miranda started Freestyle Love Supreme (FLS), an improv hip-hop musical group, in 2004, and the group performed both on and off Broadway from 2004 until 2020. Freestyle, in which rappers improvise their rhymes is, according to Alim, a communal and competitive discourse; he writes: "Lyrical battling, which often occurs in the cipher, is a highly animated engagement where the Rap lyricist's skills are sharpened and presented to a critical circle of Hip-hop conscious beings" (97). The Hulu documentary *We Are Freestyle Love Supreme* (Fried, 2020) portrays Miranda's version of freestyle as more communal than competitive. Before going on stage each night, each artist shares an encouraging "I got your back" with his fellow performers (Fried, 2020). However, the elements of freestyle, including audience participation and the trading of rhymes by performers, are all present in the FLS shows, and Miranda infuses these elements into the more contentious battle songs in *Hamilton*. Referring to "Farmer Refuted," Hamilton's verbal battle with royalist Samuel Seabury, Miranda states,

> The fun (and laborious part) of this tune was having Hamilton dismantle Seabury using the same vowels and cadences and talking over him. . . . It felt like some kind of superpower Hamilton could deploy to impress his friends. (Miranda & McCarter, 2016, p. 49)

"Farmer Refuted" also represents an engaging melding of musical styles, with Hamilton rapping over Seabury's sung melody, which serves to create a battle not only in verbiage but in form as well. Miranda often mentions where his personality converges with that of his Hamilton character, and this use of freestyle to build camaraderie seems to be one such area, though Miranda does not explicitly state it in his annotations.

FLS member Andrew Bancroft describes Miranda similarly, as "our verbal gymnast. He's our poet. He's unstoppable" (Fried, 2020) a sentiment that synchronizes nicely with *Hamilton*'s Burr, who calls Hamilton "non-stop" and recounts the history of Hamilton's prolific writing in *The Federalist Papers* (Miranda & McCarter, 2016, p. 137). As Veneziale explains, FLS is a group of friends "expressing themselves and, in some small way, saying, 'I can't wait to hear what you're going to say next'" (Fried, 2020), and that is exactly what the core group of Hamilton's friends, Laurens, Mulligan, Lafayette, and even sometimes Burr do in the play. Aside from the freestyle battles in the play, the legacy of FLS appears in *Hamilton*'s casting of Daveed Diggs (Lafayette/Jefferson) and Chris Jackson (Washington), who both performed in the improv group, as well as in *Hamilton*'s direction by FLS's Thomas Kail. Fraternal dedication and love of the verbal is another way in which Miranda and Hamilton intersect, making the play an almost remix of Hamilton's and Miranda's lives, just as it remixes hip-hop and history.

Remix has long been a cultural phenomenon, and its foundational element, sampling (Navas, 2012, p. 12), allows for remixing to take place. The practice of the remix, as it involves technology, began to identify itself through the use of audio sampling and has recently "expanded to include music and sound as well as moving and static images taken from films, television, the Internet, personal archives, and elsewhere" (Knobel & Lankshear, 2008, p. 22). Hip-hop scholars point out that rap artists especially make use of technologies, such as recording technologies, turntables, and computers, in unexpected ways to sample and remix elements within their music and have done so since technologies have allowed (Rose, 1994; Banks, 2011; Dixon-Román & Gomez, 2013). In *Black Noise: Rap Music and Black Culture in Contemporary America*, Tricia Rose (1994) explains that rap music has always been driven by a culture of remix: "For rap's language wizards, all images, sounds, ideas, and icons are ripe for recontextualization, pun, mockery, and celebration" (p. 3). Today's digital culture increasingly engages in remix culture, or what Lawrence Lessig (2008) would call, a "Read/Write (RW) culture." Lessig likens the practice of remixing to another commonplace practice; he writes,

> To me, it is just like cooking. In your cupboard in your kitchen you have lots of different things and you try to connect different tastes together to create something interesting. The remix artist does the same thing with bits of culture found in his digital cupboard. (2008, p. 71)

Miranda's cupboard includes diverse bits of culture from a variety of sources including the AOL dial-up tone (Rotten Tomatoes, 2020) and classic theater—Washington's declaration that he is "the very model of a modern major general" is a line from *The Pirates of Penzance* (Miranda & McCarter, 2016, p. 61), for example—but his ability to remix is perhaps most pleasing when he uses it add to the legacy of remix and sampling in hip-hop culture. One example is the song "Ten Duel Commandments," which borrows from The Notorious B.I.G.'s (Biggie's) "Ten Crack Commandments," which in turn samples from "Vallarta" by Les McCann (Miranda & McCarter, 2016, p. 99). In sampling from Biggie, Miranda further connects the life of a founding father of the country to the life of one of rap's most influential but short-lived stars. Both Biggie and Hamilton were fatally shot but live on in their verses.

Potter (1995) states, "Rappers who sample hip-hop martyrs such as Tupac Shakur and Notorious B.I.G. add to the creation of new identities, tributes that often become part of new narratives within the imagined community of hip-hop culture" (p. 109). In simultaneously invoking the memories of Biggie and Hamilton, Miranda draws a comparison between the two men that goes beyond the biographical facts of their lives, and he raises Biggie from the dead through the sampling of his music.

Prior to the popularity of Miranda's musical, Hamilton's death was the single story that many Americans knew about him. Miranda expands his story and the reach of music like Biggie's all at once. Furthermore, in borrowing the structure of Biggie's song, Miranda, who states he, "wanted to understand that dueling was simply a way of life, with its own codes and customs" (Miranda & McCarter, 2016, p. 99), demonstrates the cultural codes that link practices like dueling and drug dealing. Both are problematic and harmful but fed by cultural narratives and inequalities that lead participants to believe they have no choice but to participate in their rituals. Through Hamilton, Miranda shows how people can gain cultural currency via following almost ritualistic rules of order; Biggie writes of the consequences of not following those rules. Though Miranda is not using turntables to execute his sampling, mashing up Biggie's story with Hamilton's turns him into a sort of DJ—a modern, digital griot. Miranda's sampling manipulates multiple layers of the narrative, from the characters to the underlying beat, to create a complex intersection of meaning.

Sampling gained prominence in the 1970s through DJs' uses of audio manipulation (Navas, 2012 p. 14). As such, it is important to understand the influence of the DJ on remix culture as it relates to modern composition practices. In his 2011 work, *Digital Griots: African American Rhetoric in a Multimedia Age*, Adam Banks conceptualizes the DJ as a digital griot. For Banks, the digital griot, borne from DJ culture, is intrinsically linked with the hip-hop culture from which it emerged and has impacted creative writing practices in a way that furthers the principles and practices of hip-hop: "Hip-hop has disrupted the notion of a linear text and . . . has placed a focus on recycling, reuse, and repurposing . . . language and tools old and new," and as such, "compositionists have settled on some of the practices of the DJ" (2011, p. 20). Banks's digital griot stems from African American rhetorical traditions that combine the art of the DJ and the storytelling of the griot to explore the writing process. Although he writes from a position specifically in reference to such remixing in digital media, the metaphor of the digital griot speaks to Miranda's writing practices as well.

As a practice, the digital griot connects infrastructures so commonly associated with the white, male hegemonic narrative to the everyday practices of African American rhetorical traditions. This is further a similar metaphor for the world of theater and Miranda's place within the theatrical world historically. Banks suggests treating such real-world applications of remixing as a process of DJing can help bridge the metaphor from the physical to the digital:

> Understanding the DJ as a current manifestation of the griot—as a digital griot—and linking the practices of the DJ to other griots throughout the tradition (the storytellers, the preachers, the standup comics, the spoken word poets, and others) will allow an approach to African American rhetoric that is fluid and forward looking yet firmly rooted in African traditions. The exemplary DJ is a model of real rhetorical agility. (2011, p. 3)

Such rhetorical agility is key to *Hamilton*. An analysis for *FiveThirtyEight* finds *Hamilton* both has significantly more words than the average musical and delivers those words at a faster pace. *Hamilton*'s cast album contains 20,520 words in two hours and 23 minutes, while the next closest, *Phantom of the Opera,* has only 6,789 words in one hour and 40 minutes (Libresco, 2015). Likewise, *Hamilton* delivers an average of 144 words per minute, while the next most verbally dense album *Spring Awakening* delivers 77 words per minute (Libresco, 2015).

The idea that griots must be rhetorically agile is not new. In 1997, Geneva Smitherman argued, "As African America's 'griot,' the rapper must be lyrically/linguistically fluent; he or she is expected to testify, to speak the truth, to come wit it in no uncertain terms" (p. 4). Thus, the modern griot is based in both digital remixing and hip-hop culture and operates through the same practices as those used in the art of the DJ, which Banks describes as "the cut, break, sample, mic, remix, mixtape, and a continual, crate-digging search that allows narrative, text, and history to continue while allowing for new voices, new arguments" (2011, p. 29)

The digital griot thus emphasizes the importance of acknowledging the place of these traditions within the digital landscape and power hierarchies. Further, the griot opens a path for diverse narratives to occur within these structures, such as the reformation of Hamilton as an everyman rather than the traditional "great man."

While this work acknowledges the foundation of hip-hop in black culture, it has clearly grown to encompass the creative interests of many cultures. Miranda himself is evidence of this. As Rose suggests, "To suggest that rap is a black idiom that prioritizes black culture and that articulates the problems of black urban life does not deny the pleasure and participation of others" (1994, p. 4). *Hamilton* uses the theater to open the door for others to participate in the culture of hip-hop and the history of the founding fathers in new ways. Miranda's maneuvering of traditional hip-hop rhetorical devices, such as freestyle and remix, allows for levels of pleasure that engage the audience across historical texts—from revolutionary America to classic rap. Employing hip-hop poetics to remix the hegemonic story of Alexander Hamilton as a "great man" into that of Hamilton as the "everyman" is an act of using voice to free the oppressed from the indoctrination of whitewashed, hegemonic historical narratives as well as the expectations of musical theater.

REFERENCES

Banks, A. (2011). *Digital griots: African American rhetoric in a multimedia age.* Southern Illinois University Press.

Campbell, K. E. (2005). *Gettin' our groove on: Rhetoric, language, and literacy for the hip-hop generation.* Wayne State University Press.

Dixon-Román, E. J., & Gomez, W. (2013). En mi barrio: Cuban youth culture and possibilities in hip-hop and reggaetón. In K. Jocson (Ed.), *Cultural transformations: Youth and pedagogies of possibility* (pp. 183–202). Harvard Education Press.

Fried, A. (Director). (2020). *We are freestyle love supreme* [Film]. Boardwalk Pictures.

Goodman, S. (2020, July 10). *Debating 'Hamilton' as it shifts from stage to screen.* New York Times. https://www.nytimes.com/2020/07/10/movies/hamilton-critics-lin-manuel-miranda.html

Isenberg, N. (2016, March 17). *Let's not pretend that 'Hamilton' is history.* Zócalo Public Square. https://www.zocalopublicsquare.org/2016/03/17/lets-not-pretend-that-hamilton-is-history/ideas/nexus

Johnson, J. (2017). *Killing poetry: Blackness and the making of slam and spoken word communities.* Rutgers University Press.

Knobel, M., & Lankshear, C. (2008). Remix: The art and craft of endless hybridization. *Journal of Adolescent & Adult Literacy, 52*(1), 22–33.

Lessig, L. (2008). *Remix: Making art and commerce thrive in the hybrid economy.* Penguin.

Libresco, L. (2015, October 5). *'Hamilton' would last 4 to 6 hours if it were sung at the pace of other Broadway shows.* FiveThirtyEight. https://www.fivethirtyeight.com/features/hamilton-is-the-very-model-of-a-modern-fast-paced-musical

Miranda, L.-M., & McCarter, J. (2016). *Hamilton: The revolution: Being the complete libretto of the Broadway musical, with a true account of its creation, and concise remarks on hip-hop, the power of stories, and the new America (First edition.).* Grand Central Pub.

Monteiro, L. D. (2016). Race-conscious casting and the erasure of the black past in Lin-Manuel Miranda's *Hamilton. The Public Historian, 38*(1), 89.

Navas, E. (2012). *Remix theory: The aesthetics of sampling.* Ambra Verlag.

Notorious B. I. G., The. (1997). Ten crack commandments [Song]. On *Life After Death* [Album]. Bad Boy, Arista.

Postlewait, T. (1991). Historiography and the theatrical event: A primer with twelve cruxes. *Theatre Journal, 43*(2), 157–178.

Potter, R. A. (1995). *Spectacular vernaculars: Hip-Hop and the politics of postmodernism.* SUNY Press.

Rose, T. (1994). *Black noise: Rap music and Black culture in contemporary America.* Wesleyan University Press.

Rotten Tomatoes [@RottenTomatoes]. (2020, July 7). *Lin-Manuel Miranda breaks down his process of writing the song, 'My Shot' for #Hamilton* [Tweet; Video]. Twitter. https://www.twitter.com/RottenTomatoes/status/1280619707893071872

Schwartz, J. M., & Cook, T. (2002). Archives, records, and power: The making of modern memory. *Archival Science, 2*, 1–19.

Smitherman, G. (1997). "The chain remain the same:" Communicative practices in the hip-hop nation. *Journal of Black Studies, 28*(1), 3–25.

Chapter 8

Kim Chi at *RuPaul's Drag Race*

Rearticulating Fatphobia, Sissyphobia, and Asianphobia in the Gay Male Community in American Context

Quang Ngo

At the grand finale of the eighth season of *RuPaul's Drag Race*, Bob the Drag Queen from New York was announced the winner in front of a packed theater. The auditorium erupted with applause, cheering enthusiastically for the charismatic queen who had just won the coveted crown.

To be named America's Next Drag Superstar, Bob the Drag Queen, Kim Chi, and Naomi Smalls were asked to lip-sync to their own original songs so that they could showcase their "charisma, uniqueness, nerve, and talent." Each sought to make one last impression on RuPaul and the audience, proving why she, and she only, deserved the title. The three lip-syncing performances could not have been more different because they underscored three completely distinctive styles of drag that Bob the Drag Queen, Kim Chi, and Naomi Smalls embodied throughout the competition. Whereas Bob the Drag Queen lip-synced to a song that emphasized her multifaceted talents and unique personality, Naomi Smalls delivered a captivating performance that highlighted her model-like physical appearance and beauty. Kim Chi utilized the occasion to perform a song that not only communicated a powerful message of empowerment but also displayed her cultural pride. Regardless of these differences, they all shared one commonality—that is, they are all members of racial minority groups, thereby indicating how diverse this batch of finalists is.

Of these three, only Kim Chi is Asian. Yet it is hard to miss that she is of Korean descent, as her drag persona is highly influenced by this cultural identity. As she additionally acknowledged in an interview, "I've always been proud of being a Korean and Korean culture, which I think is extremely beautiful. That's the reason why I named my stage persona as Kim Chi—to promote Korea" (Hong, 2017). This decision to name her drag persona after Korea's most recognized traditional dish is a strategic move on her part to showcase her marked appreciation for her Korean background, on the one hand, and to underscore her determined intent to introduce her culture to a broader public, on the other. As a result, it seems probable that she intends her drag name to serve as an homage to her heritage and, more significantly, as a self-evident identificatory marker she relies on to position herself not simply as Asian American but as Korean American once in drag. And she succeeded in presenting her drag persona as such on *RuPaul's Drag Race*.

Kim Chi had many great moments during the span of the competition in which she won two main challenges, never landed in the bottom two, and received unanimous praise for her fashion sense and makeup skills. In this chapter, I focus on the seventh episode, titled "Shady Politics," which tasks the six remaining queens to write and film "shady presidential campaign ads, throwing their wigs in the ring to become the first drag president of the USA" (*Logo TV*, 2020). This episode shows how Kim Chi renegotiates, rearticulates, and subverts a system of normative values and ideals that champion and espouse a problematic vision of a gay man this community comes to embrace in an American context. In the face of this challenge, Kim Chi decides to be political, using her presidential campaign ad to call out the workings of whiteness, dominant masculinities, and a valorization of muscularity as contributing to the reification of a prejudiced system of hegemonic expectations that come to privilege gay men who embody these physical properties and simultaneously marginalize those who do not. More rhetorically, Kim Chi delivers a social critique of the detrimental influences of these interlaced ideologies on the creation of accepted biased norms and internalized discriminatory attitudes inside/within the gay male community. Her persona clearly embodies an intersectional identity.

Following its premiere on Logo TV in 2009, *RuPaul's Drag Race* has become a cultural phenomenon. Its success is indisputable, as evidenced by its immense popularity among audiences and critics. Produced by World of Wonder, *RuPaul's Drag Race* is a reality competition television program centered on drag—that is, "a gendered habitus of the performative, one which relies on intensification to act as a parody of the naturalized limitations on desire, on bodies, and on the dressing of those bodies that occur within society" (Moore, 2013, p. 19). But there is more to drag than just a performance for entertainment purposes. Indeed, Judith Butler (1999) invokes drag as one of those exemplary performative means of de-essentializing gender and uncovering the illusion of its stability because drag queens are imbued with the capacity for reappropriating dominant gender scripts for nonconventional uses. Given its focus on drag, *RuPaul's Drag Race* provides many examples of performing gender outside of its normative context, reconfirming that gender is never a stable identity but instead is a negotiable construction that can be undone and can be subverted.

During each episode, contestants participate in three different challenges: the mini challenge, the main challenge, and the catwalk challenge. Sandwiched between these challenges are instances when the audience can witness how performers look out of drag, share their feelings and thoughts, or grasp what the challenge means for them and how they plan on delivering and performing it before a panel of judges, headed by RuPaul. Each week, the two drag queens who perform poorly in the main challenge are asked to "lip-sync for the life." Based on the lip-syncing performance, RuPaul then decides who gets to stay and who has to sashay away (Moore, 2013). At the end of each episode, RuPaul and the drag queens always utter loud and clear the inspirational mantra: "If you can't love yourself, how in the hell you gonna love somebody else? Can I have an amen up in here?" These statements come to encapsulate the message of empowerment and optimism that the show hopes to communicate to an audience who might have been marginalized for their nonnormative genders and nonconforming sexualities. Thus, *RuPaul's Drag Race* comes to play a significant role in catapulting drag into a popular form of entertainment for mainstream television consumption and a key part in promoting the visibility of drag culture.

Yet at the same time, it attracts the critical attention of scholars who remain skeptical of its normalizing takes on gender, race, or sexuality. According to González and Cavazos (2016), *RuPaul's Drag Race* may have provided the contestants with enough screen time to disclose their personal concerns and to educate the audience to a variegated array of gay-related political and health issues, thereby showing them in a more humane manner, but at the expense of stereotyping them through gender norms deeply rooted in the heteronormative system. Moreover, Edgar (2011) asserted that the first season of the show doubtless misses out on a valuable opportunity to effactually subvert hegemonic gender scripts due to its tendency to overwhelmingly give more credits to drag queens that can performatively appropriate feminine stereotypes in their drag performance as well as successfully conceal any visible residue of their male physical traits in their drag transformations. By invoking a neoliberalist lens, Goldmark (2015) additionally elucidated the way in which the first season "presents a single-axis model of social progress, where sexuality is akin to, but separable from, other realms such as race" (p. 507), eventually making possible its intent to potentially gloss over identificatory categories as distinct markers of personhood as well as to render them irrelevant in the service of promoting a false perception of inclusivity to the extent that differences do not seem to matter within American public imagination and that each contestant is offered an equal shot at winning. This line of critique spotlights the show's complicity in upholding and promoting ideologies and morals deeply embedded in the American Dream that encourages marginalized individuals to pull themselves up by their own bootstraps and to achieve better socio-economic conditions. For Strings and Bui (2014) in their study of its third season, one of the limitations of *RuPaul's Drag Race* is its quite parochial slant on depicting drag queens of color, thus failing to advance more nuanced representations of race. More specifically, contestants of color are expected to adhere to racialized images and stereotypic tropes commonly associated with hegemonic expectations. Whereas the show illuminates how to renegotiate and rearticulate gender norms and gender expectations via drag performance, it reproduces race as an essentialized, rather than constructed, marker of identification that can never be violated (Strings & Bui, 2014).

Despite such limitations, *RuPaul's Drag Race* remains a subversive space, queering the mainstream television landscape via its unapologetic celebration of drag subcultural norms and values. Over the course of its subsequent seasons, one can witness that the show and its contestants have become more attentive to, and more vocal about, a set of social and political problems inherent to the gay community. Perhaps the presidential campaign commercial created by Kim Chi in the seventh episode exemplifies one of those instances in *RuPaul's Drag Race* that proves why the show continues to function as a springboard for examining the complex nexus of discursive and ideological forces constantly shaping the dominant set of ideals, norms, and values that come to privilege a certain type of gay man and simultaneously oppress the rest in an American context. I therefore concentrate on this rhetorical artifact as an entrée to tracking the characterization of a desirable gay man and exploring its implications.

Over the course of the ten episodes on *RuPaul's Drag Race*, Kim Chi melds seamlessly her avant-garde fashion sense and her marked fascination with anime to construct a colorful, quirky, and vibrant drag character that is also remarkably shaped by her identity as Korean American. As a result, she breaks away from confining her drag persona to orientalist and racial tropes of Asian American peoples and cultures (Kornhaber, 2016). Not only does Kim Chi find a way to introduce Korean culture and to challenge dominant expectations about Asian American contestants, but she also hits upon issues gay men of color, especially gay Asian men, may encounter in American culture. The shady presidential campaign comes to exemplify this awareness of their lived experiences as deeply influenced by their sexuality and race.

The point of the main challenge is to give the contestants an opportunity to employ their comedic skills to attack a fellow queen in the form of a political ad. As a result, Kim Chi is paired with Naomi Smalls, whose drag persona reflects the feminine beauty ideal because of her physical attractiveness. Despite their shared appreciation for fashion, the stark contrast between their drag personae is remarkably evident. Whereas Naomi Smalls fits perfectly with dominant cultural and social expectations about beauty standards, the same cannot be said about Kim Chi. No wonder they approach the challenge differently even though they address the same topic. In fact, Kim Chi devotes her campaign commercial to critiquing Smalls' single-minded pursuit of beauty, and at the same time dedicates it to empowering herself and other gay men who look and act like her. The content of her ad may have been short, lasting only a minute, but it conveys a rhetorical message that illustrates a bold attempt on her part to reclaim her sense of self-worth.

Given her enthusiasm for the idea of undergoing cosmetic surgery to make one more beautiful, it is unsurprising that Naomi Smalls makes "free injectable cosmetics" the key component of her campaign. Of course, Kim Chi takes issue with Smalls' message and begins her presidential ad with an effort to slam Smalls for it. She specifically conjectures that "Naomi Smalls says, 'Beauty is pain,' but is she aware of the consequences of her actions?" In raising this question, Kim Chi seems to express a level of concern over Smalls' promise of providing injectable cosmetics for all. Because of this skepticism about the widespread use of this method to enhance one's beauty, Kim Chi wonders whether Naomi Smalls recognizes the unintended outcomes of such a promise. By directly attacking her opponent on this ground, she implies that Smalls embraces a kind of beauty highly reflective of consumerist ideals. Consumerism is a problematic concept when applied to elucidate beauty standards and body ideals because it promotes a very specific vision of physical attractiveness attainable only by the consumption of cosmetic goods and procedures. Therefore, Kim Chi finds the message Smalls hopes to send out reckless, as it reconfirms unhealthy perceptions of beauty and celebrates a kind of superficial aesthetics rooted in the consumerist model. Ultimately, she challenges Smalls' recommendation of medical and surgical techniques as the only way to improve one's physical appearance.

Once she establishes Naomi Smalls' deleterious appetite for physical perfection, Kim Chi focuses her attack on Smalls' statuesque figure. In her own words, "America is a kitchen that needs a strong chef, and never trust a skinny cook—small body, small mind." By metaphorically comparing America with "a kitchen," Kim Chi succeeds in looking for a way to portray Smalls in an unfavorable light. She intends this metaphor to establish Smalls as unfit for the job, given the notion that her skinny body is synonymous with a lack of desire to eat. To be skinny like Naomi Smalls is to avoid cooking and consuming food at all costs. For Kim Chi, then, without an appreciation for both, Naomi Smalls is rendered unqualified for the drag presidential position. She hopes that by framing her opponent as lacking qualifications and skills to effectively work in the kitchen, voters will think more carefully and more critically about supporting Smalls. As a result, Kim Chi indicates that she is not intimidated by Smalls' skinny body. She even makes fun of it when she later asserts, "She thinks she's the skinniest queen, but her waist is 22 inches? What a fat ass." Kim Chi hits upon the idea of painting the picture of Smalls' 22-inch waist as not small enough to call into question who gets to define the parameters or set the limits of what constitutes skinniness. This intent to call Naomi Smalls "a fat ass" reflects an attempt to demonstrate that one's search to become skinny will never end because one can never be satisfied with one's body frame.

Following the critique of Naomi Smalls as a superficial drag queen with an insatiable desire to look beautiful, Kim Chi explicitly claims that "Shady gays believe in 'No fats, no femmes, and no Asians.'" In making this claim, she highlights a set of three attributes that make a gay man undesirable among other gay men. Let us unpack what Kim Chi means by stating that any gay men who fall into these categories might not have been accepted within the gay community.

When it comes to the topic of how gay men perceive the ideal male body, the majority wish to develop a perfect, hyper-masculine one. For instance, Padva (2002) analyzed interviews and photos of five gay men of different sizes and shapes that were published in an editorial piece in the British magazine dedicated to gay readers, *Attitude*. These five gay men are selected to represent a variety of queer male bodies. Despite their physical differences, they all agree that the gay scene and the media both favor the male body that shows no imperfections, thus creating an illusion that a well-defined, toned, and muscular body is what the gay community prefers. Padva then concluded, "The naked issue of *Attitude* magazine, in its controversial way, criticizes the homogeneity of the (queer) male body" (p. 291). In this context, the fact that this editorial is intended as a valuable occasion to condemn how the queer male body is perceived indicates the problematic way gay men understand and construct their body images. Regardless of their shapes and sizes, most gay men can be said to be drawn more toward a "perfect," hyper-masculine body. Thus, it is understandable for Kim Chi to reveal how being fat alienates her from being welcomed into the gay community. Wood (2004) further states that "gendered body aesthetics not only constitute a pivotal dimension in the construction of gay subcultural identities, but also determine power relations both within and between subcommunities" (p. 57). The gay community determines that the rugged, muscular body should be placed at the top of the hierarchy of male beauty, thus perpetuating a desire for gay men who exemplify such aesthetic ideals. Dilts (2011) recounts a personal story of how because he is rejected by the gay community for not having the ideal body, he becomes obsessed with exercises and later develops eating disorders. His account thus provides a unique window into how the preoccupation with a perfect body leads to negative consequences. Dilts writes, "Gay and bisexual men have normalized body obsession to the point that eating disorders are an accepted and unnoticed way of life" (p. 23). Therefore, it makes complete sense for Kim Chi to point out the irrational preference for an unachievable body image that might have driven gay men away from other more meaningful activities. And to refuse another person for not having an Adonis-like body is foolish, and, as Kim Chi puts it, shady.

Along these lines, Kim Chi also criticizes how the gay community further marginalizes gay men who act femininely. Queer scholars have addressed this problem by exposing the toxic role that hypermasculinity plays in this community. Clarkson (2006) asserts that "a straight-acting gay identity is positioned in opposition to cultural stereotypes of gay men that conflate femininity with homosexuality" (p. 192). Apparently, straight-acting gay men believe that their gayness causes them to be viewed as less than "real" men. They are forced to develop their own ways of defining their own masculinity that might challenge such a conflation. And straight-acting gay men, in their quest to prove that their sexual orientation does not emasculate the way they act and behave, appropriate a version of working-class masculinity. This way they believe they can distance themselves from being associated with straight women's femininity and behaviors typically associated with gay men. By disapproving of feminine gay men, they simultaneously perpetuate a discriminatory system that "relegates them to a lower tier of masculinity" (p. 205). As Eguchi (2011) acknowledges, straight-acting gay men become sissyphobic—a phobia that makes it possible for them "to justify and empower their masculinity" (p. 38). Thus, straight-acting gay men internalize homophobia and consider it acceptable to discriminate against feminine gay men. In other words, they subconsciously adhere to cardinally established binary gender expectations. They do not see any options other than to cultivate a masculine identity—one that is constantly pitted against feminine gay men. To reiterate, straight-acting gay men deny the existence of feminine gay men because hegemonic masculinity is deeply ingrained in their identity construction, and they genuinely believe that those who do not abide by masculine traits, codes, and cues are a "failure of being men" (p. 207, Eguchi, 2009). Being conscious of this problematic situation, Kim Chi draws critical attention to gay men being shady and inconsiderate for rejecting feminine gay men. For Kim Chi, such perceptions are short-sighted. As implied in the rainbow flag, a widely recognizable symbol for the gay community, which indicates different shades of being a gay person, respect should be paid toward disparate ways of performing gay sexuality. Therefore, Kim Chi advocates self-worth by exposing the discrimination of straight-acting gay men who do not see the beauty of nonstraight-acting gay men.

Finally, Kim Chi vocalizes how gay men of Asian descent are typically marginalized within the gay community. The issue of racism against Asian men in this sexual minority group is not a new topic. Han (2006) asserts, "It is clear that race has always played an integral part of defining masculinity" (p. 84), meaning that white masculinity is contextualized as the dominant and hegemonic form. It operates to ascertain that whiteness should always be at the center, around which the gay community is structured and organized. The racial hierarchy has relegated gay Asian men to further marginalization in that they are forced into stereotypical images of femininity and submissiveness, therefore making them less desirable. Gay Asian men might consider such stereotypes as actually representing how they should behave to find a partner, leading to them being "socially conditioned to not question white male supremacy within the white-centered gay community" (Han 2007, pp. 93-94). Han additionally places the issue of race within the discourse of exclusion and discloses that gay men of color are marginalized differently. In a discussion of the forms of racism directed at gay Asian men, Han points out that they are exoticized and become interchangeable with one another. A white-centered gay community may inflict pain on gay Asian men who have internalized biased perceptions. They thus discriminate against other races, even their own race, by refusing to date other gay men of color. Han (2008) further explains how mainstream stories, told from the preferred perspectives of white gay men, consolidate white privilege and simultaneously ignore voices of the Other. In other words, the social reality of gay Asian men is shaped and constructed by those who hold the power to disseminate hegemonic and white masculinist messages and to perpetuate images that gay Asian men feed upon. Han recognizes the problem of colorblindness, allowing for the erasure of race when addressing the gay community.

Colorblindness endorses a discourse that downplays the presence of race, which in a sense maintains racial inequality and discrimination. Obasogie (2013) particularly contextualizes colorblindness as a set of ideologies dictating that "race is a social construction without any inherent biological significance" (p. 115). Colorblindness additionally presents an undeniable obstacle to open conversations regarding racial discrimination. Those who believe in colorblindness do not consider that race should be the criterion one should pay close attention to in terms of judging and understanding the Other's voice and identity. A colorblind gay community situates racism in the background and further turns this issue into something unimportant. Colorblindness encourages gay men to avoid acknowledging racial advantage, and both consciously and subconsciously contributes to the ongoing and perpetual presence of racism within this community. Clearly, race should be placed at the center of any discourse surrounding gay identity and experience, meaning that queer theory should be racialized and intersectionalized. Kim Chi makes use of the show's platform to indicate how the gay community is not as unified as it claims. It might create an illusion of unity in that it is welcoming and safe for individuals rejected from a heteronormative society that renders their sexual orientation unintelligible and unacceptable. Theoretically, oppressed people that come together to form a group cannot discriminate, thus making any discussion on this topic obsolete and impossible. Kim Chi has shown her audience otherwise, by alluding to the discrimination she encounters resulting from her racial minoritarian status.

Kim Chi recognizes that a gay male identity is constituted by the overlapping of categorial identifiers that subsequently come to determine his modes of privilege or oppression, as indicated by the following statement, "As someone who is all of the above, I understand your pain." Yet at the same time, Kim Chi reclaims her agency by boldly announcing that any gay men who disapprove of fats, femmes, and Asians are ridiculous, and in fact shady. She uses this opportunity to inform the viewer that she deserves to become the next drag president and emphasizes, "My name is Kim Chi, and say hello to yellow." Eguchi and Asante (2015) conceptualize disidentifications as a theoretical apparatus that offers gay people of color "a symbolic prism to show varying, complex, and multiple levels of identity border performances, which sometimes work within/against the normative constructions of race/gender/ sexuality" (p. 175). Applying this theoretical framework is to recognize that Kim Chi disidentifies with mainstream expectations and hegemonic ideologies associated with the gay community. She is not afraid to acknowledge that she is fat, femme, and Asian. No other gay men can deny this fact. And instead of discriminating against her, it is much more effective to get accustomed to someone who possesses all these three physical traits. Gay Asian men do exist, and they should be respected, for they are unique in their own ways. In this counter-narrative, Kim Chi constructs her identity as one that enables her to embrace her fatness, femininity, and Asianness while simultaneously revealing that she has the agency to resist dominant views of a fat gay Asian male. Han (2010) writes, "Stigmatized individuals are well aware of their stigmatized statuses and the cause of the stigmatization" (p. 85). Kim Chi understands just that. And she successfully develops coping techniques and mechanisms to handle the discriminatory situation she is in. In her political campaign, Kim Chi courageously flips the script, actively cultivates agency, proudly acknowledges that fat, femme, and Asian are indeed beautiful, and demonstratively criticizes gay men who think otherwise.

The gay community is believed to constitute individuals of disparate shape, size, and color that share one common trait—an attraction to people of the same sex. Others would have thought that members of an oppressed group without power can never discriminate against one another. But they have been wrong. Gay Asian men's experiences in American culture have disclosed how discrimination and inequality in terms of power and privilege do happen and do run rampant within their own community.

Utilizing Kim Chi's political campaign as a window, I have demonstrated how a gay Asian man, self-identified as being fat and feminine, understands racism and many other forms of discrimination within a community that should have allegedly and supposedly embraced each of its own members. *RuPaul's Drag Race*, with its huge popularity and dedicated followers, thus has clearly provided Kim Chi with a platform to construct her own counter-narratives to destabilize, challenge and rearticulate mainstream expectations of gay men who are not white, thin, and masculine.

Kim Chi is not afraid to be herself and willingly calls out the racist, fat-phobic, and sissy-phobic system of homosexuality. In the same vein, she exposes the irony of being a member of a sexual minority group that does not sympathize or understand the lived experiences nor the sexual and racial identities of gay Asian men.

However, Kim Chi does not allow these negativities to deter her from being recognized and to stop her from expressing her own identity. She embraces the agency that she has and therefore has risen above obstacles to illustrate that it is possible to navigate through marginalization and alienation. In her sit-down interview with RuPaul during the finale of the show in front of a live audience, when asked about her own vision of America's Next Drag Superstar, Kim Chi cleverly acknowledged, "And it would mean that anybody who's ever felt like they weren't part of anything, anybody that felt like they couldn't be anything, as long as you stay true to who you are, be creative, be original and your dream will come true." Being fat, being femme, and being Asian are how Kim Chi constructs her own identity. Indeed, Kim Chi proudly treasures these traits. Kim Chi exemplifies an unapologetic gay Asian person who considers fatness, femininity, and Asian-ness as what makes her not only beautiful but unique as well. In the end, Kim Chi manages to challenge hegemonic perceptions of what an ideal gay man should be like in the gay community.

REFERENCES

Butler, J. (1999). *Gender trouble: Feminism and the subversion of identity*. Routledge.

Clarkson, J. (2006). "Everyday Joe" versus "Pissy, Bitchy, Queens": Gay masculinity on StraightActing.com. *Journal of Men's Studies*, *14*(2), 191–207.

Dilts, J. (2011). Eating disorders: The gay connection. *The Gay & Lesbian Review Worldwide*, *18*(4), 23–25.

Edgar, E. (2011). *Xtravaganza!*: Drag representation and articulation in *RuPaul's Drag Race*. *Studies in Popular Culture*, *36*(1), 133–146.

Eguchi, S. (2009). Negotiating hegemonic masculinity: The rhetorical strategy of "straight-acting" among gay men. *Journal of Intercultural Communication Research*, *38*(3), 193–209.

Eguchi, S. (2011). Negotiating sissyphobia: A critical/interpretive analysis of one "femme" gay Asian body in the heteronormative world. *Journal of Men's Studies, 19*(1), 37–56.

Eguchi, S., & Asante, G. (2016). Disidentifications revisited: Queer(y)ing intercultural communication theory. *Communication Theory, 26*(2), 171–189.

Goldmark, M. (2015). National drag: The language of inclusion in *RuPaul's Drag Race. GLQ-A journal of lesbian and gay studies, 21*(4), 501–520.

González, J. C., & Cavazos, K. C. (2016). Serving fishy realness: Representations of gender equity on RuPaul's Drag Race. *Continuum: Journal of Media & Cultural Studies, 30*(6), 659–669.

Han, C. (2006). Being an Oriental, I could never be completely a man: Gay Asian men and the intersection of race, gender, sexuality, and class. *Race, Gender & Class, 13*(3/4), 82–97.

Han, C. (2007). They don't want to cruise your type: Gay men of color and the racial politics of exclusion. *Social Identities, 13*(1), 51–67.

Han, C. (2008). No fats, femmes, or Asians: The utility of critical race theory in examining the role of gay stock stories in the marginalization of gay Asian men. *Contemporary Justice Review, 11*(1), 11–22.

Han, C. (2010). One gay Asian body: A personal narrative for examining human behavior in the social environment. *Journal of Human Behavior in the Social Environment, 20*(1), 74–87.

Hong, D. Y. (2017, Jul. 14). *Drag queen Kim Chi hopes to spread Korean culture to world.* Asiaone.com. https://www.asiaone.com/showbiz/drag-queen-kim-chi-hopes-spread-korean-culture-world

Kornhaber, S. (2016, May 19). *The fierceness of 'Femme, Fat, and Asian.'* The Atlantic. https://www.theatlantic.com/entertainment/archive/2016/05/kim-chi-rupauls-drag-race-femme-fat-asian-c-winter-han-interview-middlebury/483527

Logo TV. *RuPaul's Drag Race.* http://www.logotv.com/episodes/6zvhzq/rupauls-drag-race-shady-politics-season-8-ep-807

Moore, R. (2013). Everything else is drag: Linguistic drag and gender parody on *RuPaul's Drag Race. Journal of Research in Gender Studies, 3*(2), 15–26.

Obasogie, O. K. (2013). *Blinded by sight: Seeing race through the eyes of the blind.* Stanford University Press.

Padva, G. (2002). Heavenly monsters: The politics of the male body in the naked issue of *Attitude* Magazine. *International Journal of Sexuality & Gender Studies, 7*(4), 281–292.

Strings, S., & Bui, T. L. (2014). "She Is Not Acting, She Is:" The conflict between gender and racial realness on *RuPaul's Drag Race. Feminist Media Studies, 14*(5), 822–836.

Wood, M. J. (2004). The gay male gaze: Body image disturbance and gender oppression among gay men. *Journal of Gay & Lesbian Social Services: Issues in Practice, Policy & Research, 17*(2), 43–62.

Chapter 9

Framing the Democratic Socialists of America?

National and Local Information Flows in Media Coverage of Alexandria Ocasio-Cortez

Maha Bashri

Alexandria Ocasio-Cortez (or AOC, as she is known to many) has quickly risen to political prominence in the last few years. She is the youngest woman to ever serve in Congress, winning her seat at the age of 29. While she is considered part of the Democratic Party, AOC represents the Democratic Socialists of America (DSA), which has a far more progressive and left-wing agenda than the Democratic Party. AOC, along with Michigan's Rashida Tlaib, are among the first members of the DSA to serve in Congress. Historically, Socialists in Congress are a rare but not a nonexistent phenomenon (Isserman, 2018). Ocasio-Cortez advocates a progressive platform that includes free college tuition, a Green New Deal, universal healthcare for all, and abolishment of the U.S. Immigration and Customs Enforcement (ICE).

AOC first drew national attention when she won the Democratic primary for New York's Congressional District 14 on June 26, 2018. Her victory was viewed as a huge upset because she defeated 10-term Democratic incumbent Joe Crowley. It signaled a shakeup for establishment Democrats. AOC went on to defeat Republican candidate Anthony Pappas in the general election in November 2018. She was reelected in November 2020 when she defeated Republican candidate John Cummings.

Ocasio-Cortez represents New York's 14 Congressional District (which includes part of the Bronx and Queens), one of the poorest districts in the state. Hispanics account for 46.9% of the population in the District, followed by whites at 46.5%, Asians at 16.5%, and finally blacks at 11.4%. The

District is one of the most diverse and youngest in the United States with 45.6% of its residents born outside the United States and a median age of 36.9 years (United States Census Bureau, 2018). The unemployment rate for residents is significantly higher (9%) than the national rate (6.3%) (United States Census Bureau, 2018). Only 24.6% NY Congressional District 14 residents are college graduates (United States Census Bureau, 2018). The demographic indicators reflect an ethnically diverse area with one of the lowest median household incomes ($60,173) in the state of New York and a higher percentage of people than the national average living below the poverty line (United States Census Bureau, 2018). The national average is at 13.1% while New York's 14 Congressional District is at 15.3%.

AOC won 78.2 % of the general election votes in 2018 and 71.6% in 2020. The argument has been made that her Latino heritage might have gained her the votes of fellow Latinos in the District. However, as outlined earlier, while Latinos comprise the majority of residents in the District, they account for 46% of the total population. More than 30% of residents from other ethnicities cast their votes in favor of AOC, enabling her to pull such large margins in the 2018 and 2020 general elections (Ballotpedia, 2020).

AOC's victory by these large margins also indicates that perhaps there is a shift in the electorate's views toward socialist principles in general and the DSA in particular. The DSA is a socialist labor-oriented nonprofit organization that includes members whose ideological views range from social democracy to democratic socialism (Otterbein, 2017). The organization was conceived in 1982 when its founder Michael Harrington wove together two small groups, the New American Movement and the Democratic Socialist Organizing Committee, which were remnants of the 1960s antiwar movement. Harrington was cognizant that the American public had a low opinion of Socialists, writing them off as "a small band of nuts" while not taking socialist ideologies seriously. He wanted to establish the DSA as an independent and relevant coalition of the left that would work both inside and outside of the Democratic Party—what he called a "friendly socialist lobby" (Heyward, 2017).

For most of its 35-year history, the DSA was an obscure and small political group; however, its membership grew exponentially in November 2020 to 86,000 members, and its local chapters expanded to 181 national chapters (Svart, 2020). The median age for its membership in 2017 was 38 years compared to 68 in 2013 (Heyward, 2017). Today the DSA is the largest socialist organization in the United States. Along with AOC's and Tlaib's wins in 2018, the DSA has gained two more Congressional seats when Cori Bush and Jamaal Bowman were elected in November 2020.

An understanding of the political process in democracies is mediated through information sources. Sources range from other people they discuss politics with to the media. The media, particularly the press, is a regularly used source of information (Dalton et al., 1998). This intermediary role is of particular importance during elections. The typical voter is more likely to read and pay attention to a local newspaper to better understand a candidate's policy positions than to meet them in person. Consequently, the press becomes an important conduit of information during election time. The press not only reports on the policy positions of candidates, but it also gives cues about their personal qualities and abilities (Dalton et al., 1998). Voters make decisions based on this mediated information.

Local newspapers tend to be more attuned to issues related to the communities that they serve. The viewpoints and policy perspectives of local communities, especially those of ethnic groups, come from these smaller newspapers (Hatcher, 2017). Historically local newspapers are known to build a sense of community and trust in the democratic process. It is through the lens of their stories and editorials that an agenda for debate on important public policy issues is set (Abernathy, 2014). Residents in a community rely on local newspapers to provide them with critical information needed in order for them to make informed decisions on issues pertaining to their quality of life (Friedland et al., 2012). Furthermore, government officials and candidates rely on local newspapers to inform community members of important issues on the public agenda. Local newspapers amplify important issues pertaining to the communities they serve (Cavanah, 2016). Media exposure, especially to local outlets, has been linked to increases in political deliberation and civic engagement by community residents (McLeod et al., 1999). Citizens who use news media are more likely to participate in political discourse and engage within their communities than those who do not consume local media (Filla & Johnson, 2010; McLeod et al., 1999; Scheufele et al., 2002; Stamm, 1985; Viswanath et al., 1990).

Shaw and Sparrow conclude in their 1998 study on news congruence that small media outlets (what they termed outer ring media) do not necessarily receive their cues on coverage of political issues from the elite or inner ring media. They argue that news media in the United States is not one aggregate that is monolithic in its coverage. Previous research pointed to a singular news media that takes cues from elite outlets (Grossman & Kumar, 1981; Schudson, 1982; Sigal, 1973; Sparrow, 2006). The prevalent theory for a long time was that during conditions of uncertainty (e.g., elections), reporters rely on respected colleagues and news outlets to determine issue salience news reporting cues related to them (Crouse, 1973, Grossman & Kumar, 1981; Gans, 1979; Hess, 1981). Shaw and Sparrow critiqued this approach because it treats the media as a single actor while ignoring its diversity in both the issues it covers and the audiences it caters to. For the most part, only a few studies (see Graber, 1993; Just et al., 1996; Patterson, 1980) go beyond examining a limited number of elite media outlets, after which they make a blanket assessment regarding the media's uniformity and coherence. Shaw and Sparrow make several strong arguments against the perception that the media is a single actor. First, it is always assumed that news media are all equivalent, thereby assuming institutional coherence; second, the emphasis on limited samples from elite media may lead to a bias in the findings and unwarranted generalizations; third, news reporting may vary according to distinct local and regional contexts that may present a divergence from large national newspapers.

Newspapers (local and national) are typically the locus for breaking down complex political news and public policy issues (Robinson & Davis 1990; Shaw & Sparrow, 1998). Local newspapers serve as an intermediary between small town communities and large-scale publications. National and state newspapers in the United States rely on local papers to initially report on events that later become state and national headlines (Abernathy, 2014). The U.S. mainstream media does not extensively cover the concerns and perspectives of local communities; it is these smaller local newspapers that provide cues to large-scale newspapers (Biswas & Kim, 2020). The typical voter is more likely to read and pay attention to a local newspaper with limited circulation than larger national publications. Consequently, local news coverage is of great importance in local and Congressional races because constituents get their cues from it, cues that may vary considerably from mainstream media. Thus, to assess the information provided by the media, especially during local and Congressional elections, one needs to evaluate a sample of newspapers that represent the range of American media (Dalton et al., 1998). Furthermore, there is evidence to suggest that for specific local issues the national and local media agendas will be *less* similar because local media have a special role in covering local issues (Hester & Gibson, 2007; Yopp & McAdams, 2003).

The news media can offer a range of perspectives on policy issues and politicians. Local media can frame, highlight, and interpret issues in relation to the communities that they serve, the same way national media does for broader audiences (Bleich, 2007; Lawrence, 2000). This news framing of issues gives precedence to some policy issues over others (Iyengar, 1991). News framing serves as an interpretive device that advances the "significance of an issue in the context of a community or citizens in general" (Biswas & Kim, 2020, p. 352). However, Biswas and Kim (2020) argue that the depth of coverage can vary between mainstream and local and/or ethnic media and is contingent on the issue's salience among their respective audiences. Rasmussen (2014) in her study of mainstream and ethnic media's coverage of the Affordable Care Act (ACA) concluded that differences in news framing between them led their respective audiences to have contrasting understandings of disparities in healthcare. Biswas's (2014) study had similar findings where mainstream media focused more on the general political effects of the ACA while Latino media focused more on the implications of healthcare reform for Latinos.

Studies on news media coverage of politics and politicians tend to utilize framing analysis because how a message is presented about public policy issues may shape audience perceptions (Iyengar, 1991).

Framing analysis has been central to understanding media coverage because it emphasizes the choice and depiction of characteristics of certain issues or topics (Tuchman, 1978; Tankard et al., 1991) defined framing as "the central organizing idea for news content that supplies context and suggests what the issue is through the use of selection, emphasis, exclusion and elaboration" (p. 3). Framing suggests that media frames can influence how audiences perceive issues based on the coverage. It has been used to examine different types of issues such as global warming (see for example McComas & Shanahan, 1999), controversial scientific issues such as stem cell research (e.g., Nisbet et al., 2003), healthcare (e.g., Shih et al., 2008), and political issues, the focus of this study (Gamson & Modigliani, 1989; Iyengar & Simon, 1993; Noelle-Neumann & Mathes 1987; Price & Tweksbury, 1997; Schefuele, 2000).

One of the most prevalent definitions was introduced by Entman, who asserts that frames "call attention to some aspects of reality while obscuring other elements, which might lead audiences to have different reactions" (Entman, 1993, p. 55). The way a problem is framed might determine how people understand and evaluate the issue. One of the most popular definitions of framing suggests that it is the selection of a perceived reality "in such a way as to promote a particular definition, causal interpretation, moral evaluation, and/or treatment recommendation for the item described" (Entman, 1993, p. 52). Entman (1991) also argues "news slant significantly influences public opinion" (p. 156). This has led to two categories of definitions that have evolved; the first defines frames in terms of their effects on audiences while the second set of definitions has focused on what constitutes a frame.

Gamson and Modigliani (1989) have focused on what constitutes a frame. They stress that every policy issue has a culture in which the discourse evolves and changes over time, providing different interpretations or packages. "A package has an internal structure. At its core is a central organizing idea, or *frame,* for making sense of relevant events, suggesting what is at issue (Gamson & Modigliani, 1989, p. 3). Hackett (1984) asserts that frames are linked to ideology, which he defines as "a system of ideas, values, and propositions which is characteristic of a particular social class" (p. 261).

How options are framed influences decision making by the public. Studies have shown that different wording of examples leads people to make choices differently (Machina, 1987). If a situation is presented to a person in terms of losses, the decision made by that person is very different if it is presented to that person in terms of gains (Machina, 1987). The framing of news stories may also have more subtle, and powerful, influences on audiences than bias in news stories (Pan & Kosicki, 1993). Audience members may be able to detect bias in a story, but it is hard for them to detect framing. The way an issue is presented or framed in the media will affect how the public will perceive it (Iyengar & Simon, 1993). Coverage of issues in the media has been linked to public opinion where in the salience of issues in the media agenda leads to salience of the issues in the public agenda. How the media covers an issue could have a cognitive influence on what the public thinks about the issue (Ghanem, 2002).

Framing research examining news coverage related to political issues has unveiled common patterns of coverage using the horserace frame, or focus on who was ahead, whether the issue was a local city council race or healthcare reform (Nielsen, 2013). McCombs, Lopez-Escobar, and Llamas (2000) found that the most common frames in election coverage focus on issues/ideology, perceived candidate qualifications, personality, and biography. Iyengar (1991) purports that news coverage of issues can be either through thematic or episodic frames. The episodic news frame focuses on specific events or issues without giving any attention to relevant background information that will enable audiences to better understand the issue/s under examination. Thematic frames give relevant background information that will then place an issue in general context for audiences. Iyengar (1991) found that thematic frames in news coverage are especially useful because they explain complicated and ambiguous issues when public knowledge and perhaps interest are low (political discourse). Conversely, episodic frames are more personal with less emphasis on background information.

The relationship between the press and female politicians has been a contentious one for the most part. As Ross (2004) contends there is a dissonance between the news media rhetoric, which claims to be impartial, and the actual experiences of female politicians. Patterns of stereotypical representations of female politicians have not shifted much despite the fact that more women are actively engaging in politics (Soothill & Walby 1991; Creedon 1993; Ross & Sreberny-Mohammadi 1997; Carter et al., 1998). News discourses have yet to shed the gendered approach to covering women politicians and candidates. This gendered discourse exists not only in campaign terms but as an everyday occurrence (Ross, 2002). Framing female politicians in ways that focus more on their personal attributes rather than their policy attributes renders them as less serious or perhaps even irrelevant (Carlin & Winfrey, 2009; Thomas & Wilcox, 2014). Norris (1997) concludes that even when female politicians have considerable power and global recognition (e.g., Golda Meir, Indira

Gandhi, and Margaret Thatcher) the media tends to view them through a "sex stereotyped lens."

Several studies have explored the media's actual role in framing politicians based on attributes such as gender, party affiliation, education, race, and religion (Bashri, 2019; Kahn & Goldenberg 1991; Terkildsen, 1993). However, what remains unclear is the cause-and-effect relationship between exposure to media frames and actual voters' decisions. Ross (2004) argues that most of the media is more likely to reinforce existing attitudes than to change them. Women candidates and politicians are covered by the news media in similar ways that women and women's issues are. They are relegated to lesser value and legitimacy in media discourses than their male counterparts (Bystrom, 2006; Kahn, 1994). Many studies have shown that news coverage has focused on female candidates' personalities and biographical information rather than focusing on their qualifications or positions on issues (Aday & Devitt, 2001; Devitt, 2002; Major & Coleman, 2008). The media coverage of female candidates running for office in national political races has framed their gender as a hindrance (Braden, 1996). Studies have also pointed out that news coverage story frames are more rooted in reference to race when the candidates are minorities (Caliendo & McIlwain, 2006; Major & Coleman, 2008).

When media discourses pay attention to these candidates' issue positions, they tend to frame them as "feminine" issues such as healthcare rather than as "masculine" issues such as budget or employment" (Carlin & Winfrey, 2009, p.4). Banwart et al. (2003) found that during election times male candidates received more coverage on feminine issues than they did during the primary. Consequently, male candidates are associated with both masculine and feminine issues, making them look like well-rounded candidates, unlike their female counterparts.

The increasing numbers of minority female candidates and rising political stars in U.S. politics make it necessary to examine not only gender but other attributes such as race, class, and religion. Intersectionality, as articulated by Crenshaw (1989, 1990), examines identity through axes of race and gender where both are "mutually constituted and mutually constitutive" (Ward, 2016, p. 318).

Media discourses tend to have a unitary approach in covering female candidates with multiple overlapping identities. These candidates can have one identity but not necessarily the others. Political narratives about these candidates will examine one category, be it gender or race, but not at the same time (Nielsen, 2013). It is necessary not only to examine categories such as race, gender, and class as separate categories but to understand the interrelations between them (Nielsen, 2013). Intersectional frames in both media studies and news discourses are important because identity categories, especially gender and ethnicity, cannot be separated (Collins, 2000; Crenshaw, 1990;

Hancock, 2007). An intersectional approach to understanding media frames fills a vacuum and reflects a clearer picture of how female candidates and politicians are portrayed (Nielsen, 2013).

Media research has rarely taken an intersectional approach to the examination of intersectional effects of a candidate's race and gender on the mediation of political campaigns (Ward, 2016). Gershon's 2012 study is one of the first to analyze coverage of African American and Latina Congressional female representatives. The findings indicate that these two groups received less frequent and more negative coverage than other groups of women in Congress.

This research seeks to examine the type of news frames and the intersectional categories used to cover AOC in *The Washington Post* and the *Bronx-Times Reporter*.

Against this backdrop, the study proposes the following research questions:

RQ1: What news frames were prevalent in news coverage of AOC in *The Washington Post* and the *Bronx Times-Reporter*?

RQ2: What intersectional attribute was privileged in the news coverage?

RQ3: Will news frames used to cover AOC be more episodic or thematic in local and national newspapers?

The following research seeks to examine local media coverage of Alexandria Ocasio-Cortez and compare it to the coverage of *The Washington Post. The Washington Post* has been selected because it is the most circulated newspaper in the Washington metropolitan area, home to many powerbrokers in the U.S. government. It is a leading U.S. newspaper ranked among the top 10 in terms of circulation (Agility PR, 2021). The local newspaper used for this analysis is the *Bronx Times-Reporter* (a weekly paper covering news from the Bronx, Alexandria Ocasio-Cortez's district). The author selected the *Bronx Times-Reporter* because it published news in English and therefore catered to a wide range of readers in AOC's District. The analysis period extended from June 26, 2018 (the day AOC won her first Democratic primary) to November 5, 2020 (two days after the 2020 general election). The study examined frame patterns as well as intersectional categories in local and national news coverage of Alexandria Ocasio-Cortez.

The news articles were coded by the author and a student who received extensive coding training. The sample size was 146 news articles; 75 articles were published in *The Washington Post* and 71 articles were published in the *Bronx Times-Reporter*. The unit of analysis was the entire article. The entire article as a unit of analysis gives a better understanding of the frames used. The coders selected articles that primarily focused on AOC. News frames, metaphors, and intersectional categories (gender, race, class) were closely examined by the coders. The intercoder reliability on 25% of the samples was 0.86 using Cohen's kappa.

The study is based on well-established frames used to analyze coverage of political candidates and politicians: horserace, issues/ideology, integrity, and perceived qualifications (McCombs et al., 2000). The horserace frame is defined as articles that focused on who supported or opposed AOC (without a substantive focus as to why). The issues/ideology frame is defined as articles that focused on her policy positions. The perceived qualifications frame was defined as news coverage that focused on AOC's educational and professional credentials. The integrity frame is defined as articles that focused on her consistency on policy issues and socialist views that she espouses. The research also looked at which intersectional category/ies or attribute/s was/were employed to define AOC in the news frames. The frames were further examined to determine if they were episodic or thematic.

The framing of AOC differed significantly between *The Washington Post* and the *Bronx Times-Reporter. The Washington Post* largely framed AOC in terms of who opposed her and who supported her by employing horserace frames. The *Bronx-Times Reporter* frames focused primarily on AOC's policy positions and their impact on her District. *The Washington Post* frames did examine AOC's policy positions closely but tended to frame them within the context of her "left-wing" political ideology.

RQ1 analyzed the news frames in the two publications to determine which ones were the most used. The most prevalent frame in *The Washington Post* coverage was the horserace one, where AOC's opponents and proponents are an integral part of the news story (see table 9.1). The *Bronx-Times Reporter* news frames in the articles that were examined focused more on how the ideology and issues frame policy positions. The horserace frame was used in the local news coverage, but it was most prevalent during election periods, unlike *The Washington Post* that used the frame whether it was election time or not. The least utilized frame in both newspapers was the perceived qualifications. The integrity frame was more favored in the *Bronx-Times Reporter* coverage than it was in *The Washington Post.*

RQ2 examined the intersectional categories privileged in the news coverage (see table 9.2). The study focused on gender, race, and class. Class was

Table 9.1   News Frames in *The Washington Post* and the *Bronx Times-Reporter*

The Washington Post		Bronx Times-Reporter	
Frames	*% of Frames*	*Frames*	*% of Frames*
Horserace	42	Horserace	30
Issues/Ideology	33	Issues/Ideology	41
Integrity	12	Integrity	16
Perceived Qualifications	8	Perceived Qualifications	10
Other	5	Other	3

Table 9.2   Intersectional Category Usage in *The Washington Post* and the *Bronx Times-Reporter* Articles

The Washington Post		Bronx Times-Reporter	
Intersectional Category Coverage	*% in*	*Intersectional Category Coverage*	*% in*
Gender	33	Gender	25
Race	24	Race	28
Class	29	Class	34
Other or No Category	14	Other or No Category	13

examined through the lens of AOC's policy positions and her background (economic and familial). Local news coverage focused predominately on AOC's policy positions, her own personal experiences, and their connection to her constituents. *The Washington Post* focused mostly on AOC's gender, but her class was covered extensively in the news articles. Race was covered at about the same percentage in both newspapers. Surprisingly race/ethnicity was less prevalent in the coverage coming in third after both AOC's gender and class.

RQ3 examined the use of episodic versus thematic frames. For the most part, both newspapers used episodic frames in their coverage of AOC (see table 9.3). Even when *The Washington Post* and the *Bronx Times-Reporter* focused on issue/policy frames, the news articles resorted less to the usage of thematic frames. Episodic frames present an issue by offering a specific example or metaphor. Journalists tend to use more episodic frames because they feel they believe that they make a story more compelling and digestible for readers (Gross, 2008). Conversely, thematic frames give in-depth background information about a specific issue. Journalists tend to believe that they are less engaging to their readers.

The episodic frames in both *The Washington Post* and the *Bronx Times-Reporter* employed metaphors such as young, millennial, tech-savvy to describe AOC. For example, both newspapers covered AOC reaching out to young voters by playing "Among Us" on her Twitch Channel. While the issue covered in the news articles was a serious one, getting young voters politically engaged and to the polling stations on November 3, 2020, the focus in

Table 9.3   Use of Episodic versus Thematic Frames in *The Washington Post* and the *Bronx Times-Reporter*

The Washington Post		Bronx Times-Reporter	
Intersectional Category Coverage	*% in*	*Intersectional Category Coverage*	*% in*
Episodic	85	Episodic	92
Thematic	16	Thematic	8

both publications was on the influencers and gamers who joined AOC. In another news story in *The Washington Post*, the focus was a "poetic reunion" between AOC and her second grade teacher on Twitter. The story is an emotional tribute, but has no relevance in the grand scheme of what AOC is or is not accomplishing as a Congressional representative.

The findings point to a significant usage of issue/ideology frames both publications' news coverage of AOC. This is quite interesting, since most of the literature on news coverage of female candidates and politicians overwhelmingly indicates that the focus is on perceived qualifications, appearance, and gender as a hindrance rather than their policy positions. The media does not accord female politicians the same seriousness in news coverage as it does their male counterparts. News coverage of female politicians has an anticipated set of news frames and structure. It is beyond the scope of this research to ascertain why the patterns are different in covering AOC, but it can be argued that in the local newspaper constituents are interested to know what she will, can, and has accomplished for them; therefore, there is more of a focus on issue/ideology frames. *The Washington Post* is the news outlet where power brokers get their information. AOC with her socialist positions presents an anomaly for a set of readers used to establishment politics that rarely sways from standardized norms, for both the Democratic and Republican parties. Regardless of what the reason might be, the significant use of issue/ideology frames better positions the DSA (as well as other outlier political organizations) as a viable political player in a two-party system.

Both *The Washington Post* and the *Bronx Times-Reporter* did not focus on AOC's lack of political experience. Based on the literature, the anticipated pattern of frames would focus on AOC's lack of the usual political credentials needed for Washington. AOC has little to no experience in politics prior to being elected to Congress. However, that did not become a focal frame in news coverage about her. Perhaps it is her lack of political "baggage" that forced the media to focus its attention on her policy positions. It may also be the fact that because she does not have this political baggage or "noise" trailing her, the readers are more interested in knowing what she stands for, along with what she has or has not accomplished. Ultimately, newspapers are businesses that need to cater to their readerships' interests if they are to survive.

The *Bronx Times-Reporter* focused less on AOC's gender than *The Washington Post*. The percentages can still be considered lower than usual in news coverage of female politicians. However, the national publication remained committed to the anticipated pattern of coverage. Again, it is beyond the purview of this study to determine why anticipated frames focusing on gender were used, but past research indicates that reporters in national and elite media tend to have a "pack mentality" where there is a consensus on how to cover issues resulting in established patterns of coverage (Bartels, 2020).

Race is an intersectional category that tends to be a leading frame in coverage of nonwhite candidates, but not in AOC's case. Both publications were more focused on her humble background and her class than they were on her race. The coverage discussing AOC's class emphasized how her class shaped her political ideology and policy positions.

The study's findings indicate that of the three intersectional categories (gender, race, class) examined, it was class that was at the forefront of the news coverage. This also can be connected to the large number of frames in both publications that focused on issue/ideology. I argue that this prevalence of issue//ideology frames and an emphasis on class as the main intersectional attributes indicated an interest that transcends AOC as an individual politician. She is a representative or proxy of a new ideological movement anchoring itself in American politics.

It would make great sense to test this finding further through the examination of news coverage of the other DSA Congressional members, especially Rashida Tlaib, because her tenure in Congress is similar in duration to AOC's.

The study did not seek to establish whether framing patterns were congruent in local versus national media, yet the frame patterns did provide evidence that there was a lack of congruence in coverage from both *The Washington Post* and the *Bronx Times-Reporter*, though *The Bronx Times-Reporter* was more invested in covering AOC's issue positions than *The Washington Post*. This may be attributed to the fact that its readership is comprised of AOC's constituents, which means that her positions impact their personal lives. On the other hand, *The Washington Post* placed more emphasis on horserace frames, perhaps because of the political nature of the city and the interests of the readership it serves. The local newspaper then did not depend on cues from *The Washington Post* for its coverage.

The study found that both *The Washington Post* and the *Bronx Times-Reporter* used more episodic frames than thematic ones. One would predict that with all the emphasis on issue/ideology frames, there would be in-depth explanations on AOC's policy positions, especially in *The Washington Post*. However, it seems that audiences, regardless of their education and social status, tend to favor episodic frames more than thematic ones, or perhaps journalists simply find that packaging frames as episodic makes for more compelling stories that resonate well with readers.

Overall, the research shows that while established frame patterns did manifest in the coverage many times in both publications, new coverage routines were also established. As such, there is no denying that the election of DSA candidates to Congress indicates a shift in political beliefs and ideologies in the United States. AOC's Congressional District is much younger, more ethnically diverse, and more economically impeded than most others around the country. For these groups, the current economic and political structures prevalent in the United States are not necessarily serving the needs of these constituents. Similar demographic characteristics can be found in the districts of other DSA candidates who were elected to Congress, showing that there is a pattern here. Future research would shed more concrete information on this phenomenon, but in the meantime, the DSA can revel in the fact that they are no longer considered "a small band of nuts," perhaps even becoming viable players in the American political arena.

REFERENCES

Abernathy, P. M. (2014). *Saving community journalism: The path to profitability*: UNC Press Books.

Aday, S., & Devitt, J. (2001). Style over substance: Newspaper coverage of Elizabeth Dole's presidential bid. *Harvard International Journal of Press/Politics, 6*(2), 52–73.

Agility PR. (2021, January). *Top U.S. newspapers by circulation.* https://www.agi litypr.com/resources/top-media-outlets/top-10-daily-american-newspapers/

Ballotpedia. *Alexandria Ocasio-Cortez.* (2020, December). https://ballotpedia.org/A lexandria_Ocasio-Cortez.

Banwart, M. C., Bystrom, D. G., & Robertson, T. (2003). From the primary to the general election: A comparative analysis of candidate media coverage in mixed-gender 2000 races for governor and US Senate. *American Behavioral Scientist, 46*(5), 658–676.

Bartels, L. M. (2020). *Presidential primaries and the dynamics of public choice*: Princeton University Press.

Bashri, M. (2019). Elections, representations, and journalistic schemas: Local news coverage of Ilhan Omar and Rashida Tlaib in the US Mid-term Elections. *ESSACHESS–Journal for Communication Studies, 12*(24), 129–146.

Biswas, M. (2014). Mainstream newspapers highlight politics over substance. *Newspaper Research Journal, 35*(3), 6–21.

Biswas, M., & Kim, N. Y. (2020). African American online newspapers' coverage of policy debate on the Affordable Care Act in 2017. *Newspaper Research Journal, 41*(3), 349–367.

Bleich, E. (2007). Hate crime policy in Western Europe: Responding to racist violence in Britain, Germany, and France. *American Behavioral Scientist, 51*(2), 149–165.

Braden, M. (1996). *Women politicians and the media*. University Press of Kentucky.

Bystrom, D. (2006). Advertising, web sites, and media coverage: Gender and communication along the campaign trail. In S. J. Carroll & R. L. Fox (Eds.), *Gender and elections: Shaping the future of American politics* (pp. 169–188). Cambridge University Press.

Caliendo, S. M., & McIlwain, C. D. (2006). Minority candidates, media framing, and racial cues in the 2004 election. *Harvard International Journal of Press/Politics, 11*(4), 45–69.

Carlin, D. B., & Winfrey, K. L. (2009). Have you come a long way, baby? Hillary Clinton, Sarah Palin, and sexism in 2008 campaign coverage. *Communication Studies, 60*(4), 326–343.

Carter, C., Branston, G., & Allan, S. (Eds.). (1998) *News, gender and power*. Routledge.

Cavanah, S. (2016). *Measuring metropolitan newspaper pullback and its effects on political participation* [Doctoral dissertation, University of Minnesota]. University of Minnesota Digital Conservancy.

Collins, P. H. (2002). *Black feminist thought: Knowledge, consciousness, and the politics of empowerment*: Routledge.

Creedon, P. J. (1993). *Women in mass communication* (Third Edition). SAGE Publications.

Crenshaw, K. (1989). Demarginalizing the intersection of race and sex: A black feminist critique of antidiscrimination doctrine, feminist theory and antiracist politics. *University of Chicago Legal Forum, 149*, 139–167.

Crenshaw, K. (1990). Mapping the margins: Intersectionality, identity politics, and violence against women of color. *Stanford Law Review, 43*(6), 1241–1299.

Crouse, T. (1973). *The boys on the bus*: Random House.

Dalton, R. J., Beck, P. A., & Huckfeldt, R. (1998). Partisan cues and the media: Information flows in the 1992 presidential election. *American Political Science Review, 92*(1), 111–126.

Devitt, J. (2002). Framing gender on the campaign trail: Female gubernatorial candidates and the press. *Journalism & Mass Communication Quarterly, 79*(2), 445–463.

Entman, R. M. (1991). Framing US coverage of international news: Contrasts in narratives of the KAL and Iran Air incidents. *Journal of Communication, 41*(4), 6–27.

Entman, R. M. (1993). Framing: toward clarification of a fractured paradigm. *Journal of Communication, 43*(4), 51–58.

Filla, J., & Johnson, M. (2010). Local news outlets and political participation. *Urban Affairs Review, 45*(5), 679–692.

Friedland, L., Napoli, P., Ognyanova, K., Weil, C., & Wilson III, E. J. (2012). *Review of the literature regarding critical information needs of the American public*. Unpublished manuscript. Retrieved from https://transition.fcc.gov/bureaus/ocbo/Final_Literature_Review.pdf

Gamson, W. A., & Modigliani, A. (1989). Media discourse and public opinion on nuclear power: A constructionist approach. *American Journal of Sociology, 95*(1), 1–37.

Gans, H. J. (1979). The messages behind the news. *Columbia Journalism Review, 17*(5), 40.

Gershon, S. (2012). When race, gender, and the media intersect: Campaign news coverage of minority congresswomen. *Journal of Women, Politics & Policy, 33*(2), 105–125.

Ghanem, S. (2002). Filling in the tapestry: The second level of agenda setting. In M. McCombs, D. Shaw & D. Weaver (Eds.), *Communication and democracy exploring the intellectual frontiers in agenda-setting theory* (pp. 25–37). Lawrence Erlbaum Associates.

Graber, D. A. (1993). *Processing the news: How people tame the information tide.* University Press of America.

Gross, K. (2008). Framing persuasive appeals: Episodic and thematic framing, emotional response, and policy opinion. *Political Psychology, 29*(2), 169–192.

Grossman, M. B., & Kumar, M. J. (1981). Milton's army: The white house press corps. *Political Communication, 1*(2), 145–208.

Hackett, R. A. (1984). Decline of a paradigm? Bias and objectivity in news media studies. *Critical Studies in Media Communication, 1*(3), 229–259.

Hancock, A.-M. (2009). An untraditional intersectional analysis of the 2008 election. *Politics & Gender, 5*(1), 96.

Hatcher, J. H. (2017). Don't stop the presses? The future of print and community news. *Grassroots Editor, 58*(3–4) Fall/Winter, 2–11.

Hess, S. (1981). Washington reporters. *Society, 18*(4), 55–66.

Hester, J. B., & Gibson, R. (2007). The agenda-setting function of national versus local media: A time-series analysis for the issue of same-sex marriage. *Mass Communication & Society, 10*(3), 299–317.

Heyward, A. (2017, December 21). *Since Trump's victory, Democratic Socialists of America has become a budding political force.* The Nation. https://www.the nation.com/article/archive/in-the-year-since-trumps-victory-democratic-socialists -of-america-has-become-a-budding-political-force/

Isserman, M. (2021, January 11). *Congress has more Socialists than ever before in U.S. history.* In These Times. https://www.inthesetimes.com/article/democratic-so cialism-dsa-aoc-bernie-sanders-congress

Iyengar, S. (1994). *Is anyone responsible? How television frames political issues*: University of Chicago Press.

Iyengar, S., & Simon, A. (1993). News coverage of the Gulf crisis and public opinion: A study of agenda-setting, priming, and framing. *Communication Research, 20*(3), 365–383.

Just, M. R., Crigler, A. N., Alger, D. E., Cook, T. E., Kern, M., & West, D. M. (1996). *Crosstalk: Citizens, candidates, and the media in a presidential campaign.* University of Chicago Press.

Kahn, K. F. (1994). Does gender make a difference? An experimental examination of sex stereotypes and press patterns in statewide campaigns. *American Journal of Political Science, 38*(1), 162–195.

Kahn, K. F., & Goldenberg, E. N. (1991). Women candidates in the news: An examination of gender differences in US Senate campaign coverage. *Public Opinion Quarterly, 55*(2), 180–199.

Lawrence, R. G. (2000). Game-framing the issues: Tracking the strategy frame in public policy news. *Political Communication, 17*(2), 93–114.

Machina, M. J. (1987). Choice under uncertainty: Problems solved and unsolved. *Journal of Economic Perspectives, 1*(1), 121–154.

Major, L. H., & Coleman, R. (2008). The intersection of race and gender in election coverage: What happens when the candidates don't fit the stereotypes? *The Howard Journal of Communications, 19*(4), 315–333.

McComas, K., & Shanahan, J. (1999). Telling stories about global climate change: Measuring the impact of narratives on issue cycles. *Communication Research, 26*(1), 30–57.

McCombs, M., Lopez-Escobar, E., & Llamas, J. P. (2000). Setting the agenda of attributes in the 1996 Spanish general election. *Journal of Communication, 50*(2), 77–92.

McLeod, J. M., Scheufele, D. A., & Moy, P. (1999). Community, communication, and participation: The role of mass media and interpersonal discussion in local political participation. *Political Communication, 16*(3), 315–336.

Nielsen, C. (2013). Wise Latina: Framing Sonia Sotomayor in the general-market and Latina/o-oriented prestige press. *Howard Journal of Communications, 24*(2), 117–133.

Nisbet, M. C., Brossard, D., & Kroepsch, A. (2003). Framing science: The stem cell controversy in an age of press/politics. *Harvard International Journal of Press/Politics, 8*(2), 36–70.

Noelle-Neumann, E., & Mathes, R. (1987). The event as 'event' and the event as 'news': The significance of 'consonance' for media effects research. *European Journal of Communication, 2*(4), 391–414.

Norris, P. (1997) Women leaders worldwide: A splash of color in the photo op. In Norris, P. (Ed.), *Women, media and politics* (pp. 149–65). Oxford University Press.

Otterbein, H. (2017, November 18). *The kids are all red: Socialism rises again in the age of Trump*. Philly Mag. https://www.phillymag.com/news/2017/11/18/socialism-philadelphia-millennials

Pan, Z., & Kosicki, G. M. (1993). Framing analysis: An approach to news discourse. *Political Communication, 10*(1), 55–75.

Patterson, T. E. (1980). *The mass media election: How Americans choose their president*. Praeger.

Price, V., & Tewksbury, D. (1997). News values and public opinion: A theoretical account of media priming and framing. *Progress in Communication Sciences, 13*, 173–212.

Rasmussen, A. C. (2014). Causes and solutions: Mainstream and black press framing of racial and ethnic health disparities. *Howard Journal of Communications, 25*(3), 257–280.

Robinson, J. P., & Davis, D. K. (1990). Television news and the informed public: An information-processing approach. *Journal of Communication, 40*(3), 106–119.

Ross, K. (2002). *Women, politics, media: Uneasy relations in comparative perspective*: Hampton Press.

Ross, K. (2004). Women framed: The gendered turn in mediated politics. In K. Ross & C.M. Byerly (Eds.), *Women and media: International perspectives* (pp. 60–80), Blackwell Publishing Ltd.

Ross, K., & Sreberny-Mohammadi, A. (1997). Playing house—Gender, politics and the news media in Britain. *Media, Culture & Society, 19*(1), 101–109.

Scheufele, D. A. (2000). Agenda-setting, priming, and framing revisited: Another look at cognitive effects of political communication. *Mass Communication & Society, 3*(2–3), 297–316.

Schudson, M. (1982). The politics of narrative form: The emergence of news conventions in print and television. *Daedalus, 111*(4) 97–112.

Shaw, D. R., & Sparrow, B. H. (1999). From the inner ring out: News congruence, cue-taking, and campaign coverage. *Political Research Quarterly, 52*(2), 323–351.

Shih, T.-J., Wijaya, R., & Brossard, D. (2008). Media coverage of public health epidemics: Linking framing and issue attention cycle toward an integrated theory of print news coverage of epidemics. *Mass Communication & Society, 11*(2), 141–160.

Sigal, L. V. (1973). Reporters and officials: The organization and politics of news reporting. *Mass Heath.*

Soothill, K., & Walby, S. (1991). *Sex crime in the news.* Routledge.

Sparrow, B. H. (2006). A research agenda for an institutional media. *Political Communication, 23*(2), 145–157.

Stamm, K. R. (1985). *Newspaper use and community ties: Toward a dynamic theory.* Praeger.

Svart, M. (2020, November 19). *National Political Committee newsletter — 85,000 members strong.* Democratic Socialists of America (DSA). https://www.dsausa.o rg/news/npc-newsletter-nov2020

Tankard, J., Hendrickson, L., Silberman, J., Bliss, K., & Ghanem, S. (1991, August). Media frames: Approaches to conceptualization and measurement [Paper presentation]. Annual Convention of the Association for Education in Journalism and Mass Communication (AEJMC), Boston, MA, United States.

Terkildsen, N. (1993). When white voters evaluate black candidates: The processing implications of candidate skin color, prejudice, and self-monitoring. *American Journal of Political Science, 37*(4), 1032–1053.

Thomas, S., & Wilcox, C. (2014). *Women and elective office: Past, present, and future*: Oxford University Press.

Tuchman, G. (1978). *Making news: A study in the construction of reality.* Free Press.

United States Census Bureau. *US Census Bureau: American Community Survey 5-Year Estimate 2013*-2017 (2018). https://www.census.gov/topics/public-sector/ voting.html

Viswanath, K., Finnegan Jr, J. R., Rooney Jr, B., & Potter Jr, J. (1990). Community ties in a rural Midwest community and use of newspapers and cable television. *Journalism Quarterly, 67*(4), 899–911.

Ward, O. (2016). Seeing double: Race, gender, and coverage of minority women's campaigns for the U.S. House of Representatives. *Politics & Gender, 12*(2), 317–343.

Index

Note: Page numbers in *italics* refer to tables.

About the Editors and Contributors

Jane Campbell, PhD, is professor Emerita of English, Purdue University Northwest. She received her BA from the University of Arkansas and her MA and PhD from Northern Illinois University. She is the author of *Mythic Black Fiction: The Transformation of History* (1986). Her literary criticism has appeared in *Callaloo: A Journal of African Diaspora Arts and Letters*, Obsidian; *Black Women in America*, African American Writers; *The Oxford Companion to Women's Writing in the U.S.*, the Dictionary of Literary Biography; *Heath Anthology of American Literature*, Belles Lettres; and *U.S. Media and the Middle East: Image and Perception*. Along with Theresa Carilli, she has coedited *Women and the Media: Diverse Perspectives* (2005), a special issue on women and the media for the online *Global Media Journal*, *Challenging Images of Women in the Media: Reinventing Women's Lives* (2012), *Queer Media Images: LGBT Perspectives* (with Theresa Carilli, 2013), and *Locating Queerness in the Media* (2017). She is coeditor for the Lexington Book Series, *Media, Culture, and the Arts*.

Theresa Carilli, PhD, is professor Emerita of Communication and Creative Arts, Purdue University Northwest. Her areas of concentration include media studies, performance studies, and playwriting. As a coeditor, she has published five anthologies that address media depictions of marginalized groups: *Cultural Diversity and the U.S. Media* (with Yahya Kamalipour, 1998), *Women and the Media: Diverse Perspectives* (with Jane Campbell, 2005), *Challenging Images of Women in the Media* (with Jane Campbell, 2012), *Queer Media Images: LGBT Perspectives* (with Jane Campbell, 2013), and *Locating Queerness in the Media* (with Jane Campbell, 2017). She coedited a special issue of women and the media for the online *Global Media Journal* with Jane Campbell in 2006. Currently she is coeditor of the Lexington Book series, *Media, Culture, and the Arts.* As a playwright, Carilli has published two books of plays (*Familial Circles*, 2000, and *Women as Lovers*, 1996). She edited a special theater issue of the journal *Voices in Italian Americana*, 1998. Her plays have been produced in San Francisco; San Diego; Victoria, B.C.; Melbourne, Australia; Athens, Greece; and most recently, New York City. In addition to her book *Scripting Identity: Writing Cultural Experience* (2008), which features student scripts, Carilli has published numerous articles and creative scripts. Her book *Performative Memoir: The Methodology of a Creative Process* (with Adrienne Viramontes, 2021) outlines a creative methodology which integrates performative and memoir writing. She recently published an article with the *Oxford Research Encyclopedia* entitled, "Marginalized Voices in the Global Media Dialogue" (2021).

***

Kimiko Akita, PhD, is an associate professor at Aichi Prefectural University, Japan. Dr. Akita was a dissertation fellow at the Center for Women's Intercultural Leadership at Saint Mary's College in Indiana from 2002 to 2005, as well as an associate professor at the University of Central Florida in Orlando from 2005 to 2014. She earned her PhD in Communication from Ohio University. Her research interests are in global and intercultural gender/women's studies, media studies, and pop culture.

Maha Bashri, PhD, is an associate professor of Communication at the United Arab Emirates University. Before joining UAEU, Dr. Bashri was an associate professor of Communication at Bradley University in Illinois. Her research focuses on media representations of minorities in the United States, diaspora studies, and the use of the Information Communication Technologies (ICTs) in non-Western contexts. Currently she is researching the role of media and information literacy on democratic transitions in Africa, especially in relation to networked movements (with particular reference to Sudan) and their communicative sphere.

Layla Cameron is a PhD candidate at the School of Communication at Simon Fraser University, British Columbia, Canada. Her dissertation research is focused on representations of nonnormative bodies in contemporary reality television, in addition to media production practices in the digital age. Layla also works as a journalist, filmmaker, and artist. You can read more about her work at www.laylacameron.com.

Giovanna P. Del Negro, PhD, is an associate professor of Gender Studies at Memorial University of Newfoundland. A scholar interested in the politics and aesthetics of performance, Del Negro pursues research projects that examine how issues of gender, ethnicity, class, whiteness, chronic otherness, and queerness play out in women's expressive culture, from personal experience narratives, to women's stand-up comedy, YouTube videos, and beyond. Her books include *Looking through My Mother's Eyes: Life Stories of Nine Italian Immigrant Women in Canada* and *The Passeggiata and Popular Culture in an Italian Town: Folklore and Performance of Modernity*, which was awarded the Elli Köngäs-Maranda Prize by the Women's Section of the American Folklore Society. She is a coauthor of *Identity and Everyday Life* and for five years coedited the *Journal of American Folklore*. Her work on the party records of bawdy Jewish women comics in the 1950s has been widely published. Currently, she is doing research on the drag cabaret of an Italian-Australian gay activist, which is part of a larger book project on representations of the nonna (grandmother) in the popular culture of Italy and the Italian diaspora. In addition to her professional experience as an academic, she has hosted French-language radio shows, worked with nonprofit feminist associations and heritage societies, and organized cultural festivals. She currently serves on the board of the Persistence Theatre Company, which is devoted to promoting, understanding, and embracing the core beliefs of feminism in the dramatic arts and related disciplines. She lives in St. John's, Newfoundland, Canada, with her husband, two daughters, a cat, and chickens.

Amanda Hill, PhD, is an assistant professor of Communication Studies at St. Mary's University, specializing in storytelling and media production. She has presented internationally and has published in a diverse range of journals including *Media Education Research Journal*; *Storytelling, Self, Society*; *Visual Ethnography*; *Community Literacy Journal*; and the *IAFOR Journal of Psychology & the Behavioral Sciences*. She holds a PhD in Texts and Technology from the University of Central Florida.

Michael Johnson Jr., PhD, is an associate professor of Media Theory and Criticism in the Department of Cinema and Television Arts at California State University, Northridge. His studies center on how hegemonic forces influence the depiction, adoption, consolidation, and dissemination of race, as well as human sexual identities across contemporary mass-mediated commodities like television and film

Robert Kellerman, PhD, is a professor of English at the University of Maine at Augusta, where he teaches composition, Medieval and Renaissance English literature, history of the English language, and LGBTQ Studies. His interests in the latter field include popular culture and literature, having published on Armistead Maupin and Joe Keenan. He is currently the director of the UMA's Honors Program.

Quang Ngo, PhD, is a visiting assistant professor in the Department of Communication, Media, and Performing Arts at Governors State University. His research interests lie at the intersection of critical and cultural theory, media representations and identity politics, gender and sexualities studies, and popular culture.

Sara Raffel, PhD, is an assistant professor in the English department at the University of Central Florida, where her research focuses on storytelling, technical communication, and interactivity. Her published research and digital projects appear in a wide array of publications and conferences, including Meaningful Play, Visual Ethnography, IEEE Transactions on Professional Communication, the ACM Special Interest Group on the Design of Communication, The Electronic Literature Organization, and Foundations of Digital Games.

Katrina T. Webber is a doctoral student in the Department of Communication at the University of Connecticut. She also has a Master of Science degree from Northeastern University. Her research is situated at the intersection of interpersonal and health communication, where she seeks to examine and understand communication, relational, and support-seeking behaviors of people with marginalized identities. Additionally, she is interested in the representation and perceptions of stigmatized groups in popular culture and social media. Her area of specialization focuses on weight stigma and interrogating how socially constructed ideas of health and appearance standards impact identity and relationships, and perpetuate fatphobia, racism, and health disparities.

www.ingramcontent.com/pod-product-compliance
Lightning Source LLC
Chambersburg PA
CBHW022322280326
41932CB00010B/1200